FUTU
GROW...

UNLOCKING ESTATE PLANNING AND ELDER LAW SUCCESS THROUGH MARKETING, CLIENT RELATIONS, AND TECHNOLOGY

[Handwritten notes:]
- Keyword Tools SI
- Backlinks
- Google Tag on Site Analytics
- Email: Hubspot, Mailchimp?
- Client Portal: Lawmatics Docs?
- Review Screen (Survey Monkey?)

JIM BLAKE
Founder, CEO of Bambiz

Copyright © 2024 by Jim Blake

All rights reserved. No part of this book may be
reproduced, scanned, or distributed in any printed or
electronic form without permission.

CONTENTS

INTRODUCTION 11

PART 1: MASTERING CLIENT-FOCUSED MARKETING 14
- **INTRODUCTION TO PART 1:**
  - MASTERING CLIENT-FOCUSED MARKETING 15
- **CHAPTER 1:** UNDERSTANDING YOUR AUDIENCE 19
- **CHAPTER 2:** CRAFTING COMPELLING HEADLINES AND CALLS-TO-ACTION 31
- **CHAPTER 3:** VISUAL CONTENT AND USER EXPERIENCE 43
- **CHAPTER 4:** SEO AND LOCAL SEARCH OPTIMIZATION 57
- **CHAPTER 5:** MEASURING AND IMPROVING CONTENT PERFORMANCE 79
- **WRAPPING UP PART 1:**
  - MASTERING CLIENT-FOCUSED MARKETING 89

PART 2: LEVERAGING TECHNOLOGY FOR OPERATIONAL EFFICIENCY 92
- **CHAPTER 6:** CENTRALIZED OPERATIONS FOR A SEAMLESS PRACTICE 93
- **CHAPTER 7:** ENHANCING CLIENT COMMUNICATION 107

CHAPTER 8: DATA SECURITY AND COMPLIANCE 117
WRAPPING UP PART 2: LEVERAGING
TECHNOLOGY FOR OPERATIONAL EFFICIENCY 127

PART 3: BUILDING A STRONG FIRM CULTURE 130
CHAPTER 9: THE ROLE OF FIRM CULTURE IN
CLIENT SATISFACTION 131
CHAPTER 10: MANAGING PEOPLE AND PROCESSES 145
WRAPPING UP PART 3:
BUILDING A STRONG FIRM CULTURE 161

PART 4: STAYING AHEAD WITH LEGAL TECHNOLOGY 162
CHAPTER 11: AI AND AUTOMATION IN
ESTATE PLANNING & ELDER LAW 163
CHAPTER 12: THE FUTURE OF LEGAL PRACTICE 169

PART 5: BUILDING A STAND-OUT BRAND 174
CHAPTER 13: DEFINING AND COMMUNICATING
YOUR BRAND 175
CHAPTER 14: LEVERAGING OWNED MEDIA
TO AMPLIFY YOUR MESSAGE 195

CONCLUSION: FUTURE-FOCUSED GROWTH 227
ABOUT BAMBIZ 229
ACKNOWLEDGMENTS 233

To Andrea, my rock and my biggest supporter — your love and encouragement have been everything to me as we've built our lives and this business together.

To Olivia — remember that the world is full of possibilities, and you can do anything you set your mind to. I can't wait to see all the amazing things you'll do.

To my parents — Mom and Dad, thank you for your love and support. You've taught me the values that guide me every day. To my sister — your support means the world to me. And to my nephews — watching you grow up reminds me of how important family is.

To my Bambiz team — you're not just coworkers — you're like family. I'm proud of what we've built together, and I'm thankful for each of you.

To our clients and partners — thank you for trusting us with your goals. Your belief in us is what drives everything we do.

And to everyone who has been part of this journey — thank you. This book is a reflection of all our hard work, shared challenges, and successes. Here's to the road we've traveled together and the journey still ahead.

Rave Reviews from Elder Law & Estate Planning Firms on the Strategies in This Book

Take a look at what these elder law and estate planning firms have to say about the strategies and ideas you'll discover:

"Our law firm hired Bambiz at the Pro level, and we have loved working with them! We've had great success at our events, newsletters going out on time, updating our website, social media posts happening multiple times a week, etc. We recently took on a big rebrand at our firm, and Andrea and Maren did an incredible job helping us get our message across to our clients, newsletter subscribers, and followers on social media! Highly recommend hiring Bambiz to help your firm with marketing!"

— *Silvana de Jesus (Florida)*

"Thanks to Bambiz and their incredibly caring team, I am now living my dream of conducting Estate Planning Workshops in front of packed crowds. Bambiz excels not only in workshop marketing but also in providing unwavering support every step of the way. They have expertly navigated complex Facebook issues, requiring a new page, and have completely revamped my marketing strategy. Their seamless automations and integration with my software have significantly reduced stress for my team. If you are an Estate Planning attorney, don't hesitate—Bambiz is the team you need."

— *Angela Decoteau (Louisiana)*

"Jim and his team will deliver on the results they promise. They are incredibly responsive, provide great assistance, and adjust any time it's needed. Highly recommend their services!"

— *Dan Hill (Pennsylvania)*

"I finally tried Bambiz at the recommendation of a few colleagues who have used their services to promote their educational seminars for estate planning. Bambiz did not disappoint—and actually exceeded my expectations!"

— *Deanny Lungu (California)*

"What a shift! I had been working with another social media company for promoting in-person events and just assumed that low attendance and non-qualified leads were normal. Nope—Bambiz turned all that around and was able to fill a room with qualified leads at my last event. Highly recommend!"

— *Erica Endyke (California)*

"Working with the team at Bambiz has been nothing short of a pleasure! They are efficient, responsive, and extremely knowledgeable. Additionally, they listened to what I wanted and made it happen with regards to my website. I can't thank them enough for everything they have done for my business."

— *Heidi Friedman (Florida)*

"If you are an Estate Planning and Elder Law Attorney, Bambiz is the ONLY educate-to-motivate client marketing you need. For

years, my clients have used the Bambiz proven system and have attracted and retained their ideal clients. Keep up the great work, Jim and Team. Deeply grateful for you all."

— *Molly McGrath (Colorodo)*

"I am SO happy and obsessed with our law firm's website created by Bambiz. Andrea, Jim, and the entire team really listened to what we wanted out of our website, and they completely captured our vision and brand. I would 10/10 recommend them!"

— *Lauren Klein (Florida)*

"Bambiz cares. They take the time, they focus on who you really are to make sure your content fits your firm culture. They just get it. I would highly recommend them to anyone looking for excellent marketing support for estate planning and elder law!"

— *Sarah Ostahowski (Michigan)*

Unlock Exclusive Bonus Materials

The world of marketing, technology, and client relations is always evolving. That's why we've created a collection of bonus materials designed to provide even more value beyond these pages.

By scanning the QR code below, you'll access exclusive resources, including updated strategies, training videos, and tools tailored specifically for estate planning and elder law attorneys. These materials will continue to be updated and expanded, ensuring you stay ahead of the curve in building your future-ready law firm.

https://bambiz.net/future-ready-bonus

INTRODUCTION

Welcome to *Future-Focused Growth: Unlocking Estate Planning and Elder Law Success through Marketing, Client Relations, and Technology*. I'm excited to share the exact steps that will help you not only navigate the legal industry but thrive in it. By the end of this book, you'll know how to embrace change, build a strong brand, and cultivate meaningful client relationships — all essential elements for growing a successful elder law and estate planning practice in today's world.

I know firsthand how challenging it can be to keep up with the constant evolution in the legal field. New technologies, shifting client expectations, and increased competition make it essential for firms to adapt and innovate continuously. That's why I wrote this book—to give you the knowledge and confidence to leverage the latest trends, build a brand that stands out, and engage with your clients in ways that resonate and build trust.

Before we dive into the content, let me share a bit about myself and how I came to focus on this unique area of law. My name is Jim Blake, and I'm the founder and CEO of Bambiz—a company dedicated to helping elder law and estate planning attorneys grow their practices through smart marketing and technology. My journey into this field wasn't planned, but rather a result of being in the right place at the right time—and recognizing an opportunity to make a difference. What started as simple marketing advice for a few attorneys quickly turned into a passion for helping law firms succeed in a challenging and essential area of practice.

This book is a culmination of years of experience understanding the specific needs and challenges of elder law and estate planning firms. I've had the privilege of working with many dedicated lawyers who are committed to making a positive impact in the lives of their clients. Their stories, struggles, and successes have shaped the strategies and insights I'm sharing with you here.

Throughout this book, you'll find actionable steps and real-world examples illustrating how to apply the concepts discussed. We'll explore everything from building a cohesive brand and leveraging owned media to mastering referral marketing and embracing digital transformation. Each chapter is designed to give you the tools and knowledge to enhance your practice, attract the clients you want to work with and create a firm that's prepared for the future.

As we journey together through these pages, I encourage you to think critically about your practice and how to implement these strategies to achieve your goals. Whether you're just starting or looking to take your firm to the next level, this book is here to guide you every step of the way.

Together, we'll explore the future of elder law and estate planning, and I'll help you build a firm that's not only ready for the challenges ahead but also poised to make a lasting impact.

Thank you for joining me on this journey. I'm excited to see where it takes you and how it transforms your practice. Let's get started.

PART 1:

MASTERING
CLIENT-FOCUSED
MARKETING

INTRODUCTION TO PART 1:
MASTERING CLIENT-FOCUSED MARKETING

The success of your elder law and estate planning firm hinges on more than just legal expertise. Clients today are looking for much more — they're seeking a partner who understands their challenges and can offer clear, empathetic guidance through some of life's most pivotal moments.

To truly stand out, your firm must master the art of client-focused marketing, creating an approach that aligns your message with the deep-seated needs and goals of your clients.

Consider this section your strategic playbook for creating a marketing engine that not only attracts clients but also builds long-term relationships based on trust and value.

Together, we'll explore several different "frontiers" that are key to your marketing success. These include:

Client-Forward Marketing Techniques: A deep understanding of your audience is the true "heart" of effective marketing. It's not enough to know your clients on a surface level; you need to understand their fears, their hopes, and what drives their decisions.

When you can tap into these insights, you can craft messages that resonate powerfully, positioning your firm as the clear choice in a crowded market.

Visual Storytelling and User Experience (UX): In a digital age where first impressions are often made online, the design and usability of your website play a crucial role in trust-building and client conversion. We'll explore how to use visuals and design to enhance client engagement, making your online presence a true reflection of your firm's professionalism and commitment to client care.

Search Engine Optimization (SEO): Visibility is key to success, and in today's world, that means mastering Search Engine Optimization (SEO). Whether clients are searching for elder law services or estate planning guidance, you want your firm to be at the top of their search results. In this book, we'll break down the strategies that will improve your visibility, ensuring that when potential clients are looking for services like yours, your firm is the one they find.

As you go, remember: Marketing isn't a one-and-done effort. It requires ongoing analysis, testing, and refinement to stay ahead of the curve. You'll learn how to measure the performance of your content, identify what's working, and make data-driven adjustments that keep your firm's growth on track.

CHAPTER 1:
UNDERSTANDING YOUR AUDIENCE

To build a future-focused elder law and estate planning firm, the first critical step is understanding who your clients are. This understanding is the foundation for tailoring your services and marketing efforts to meet the unique needs of your audience.

In elder law, your clients typically fall into the 60-and-above age bracket, dealing with issues related to aging or planning for the future. But here's the thing: this similarity doesn't make them a one-size-fits-all group. They come from diverse backgrounds, each with distinct needs, concerns, and goals, and recognizing that early on will encourage them not only to take the leap and engage with you but also to become long-term brand advocates.

Take John and Mary McDonald, for example. The McDonalds are a retired couple in their early 70s. They're financially comfortable, own their home, and have a modest investment portfolio. Their top priority is ensuring their assets are protected and that their estate is managed according to their wishes.

Now, contrast this with a new client, Susan White — a 65-year-old widow with limited financial resources who's worried about long-term care and Medicaid planning.

Both are elder law clients, yet their needs couldn't be more different.

Once you recognize these core differences between clients, it's time to start deep-diving — picking up key pieces of information that will ultimately help you to serve them better.

Let's start by analyzing your current client base. Use the questions below to group your clients into categories or "persona groups" and determine the next best step for each.

- Who are they?
- What are their common characteristics?
- How old are they?
- Are they married?
- What's their income and education level?

After you've got the basics, dive deeper with surveys or interviews to uncover their specific concerns, preferences, and expectations.

Beyond demographics, I also recommend that you consider psychographics — or data around your clients' values, attitudes, and lifestyles.

For example: Some clients might prioritize financial security and asset protection, while others are more focused on healthcare and long-term care planning.

By tapping into these psychographic insights, you can create marketing messages that resonate on a deeper, more personal level for each group, prequalifying their need to engage with you and appealing to their emotions, thoughts, and innate needs.

By combining the demographic and psychographic research processes, you proactively reinforce a critical aspect of client engagement: the role of trust in audience relationship-building.

In elder law and estate planning, trust is everything. Clients are entrusting you with their most personal and sensitive issues — including their finances, healthcare decisions, and family legacies.

By demonstrating a deep understanding of their demographics and psychographics from the first marketing touchpoint, you're not just offering a service — you're building a relationship based on trust and empathy. This trust is what will keep clients coming back and referring others to your firm.

Understanding your audience is not a one-time exercise; it's an ongoing commitment. For many, this commitment looks like continually revisiting your client base, re-evaluating their needs, and refining your marketing strategies accordingly.

By doing this, you'll ensure that your firm not only remains relevant but becomes a go-to resource for elder law and estate planning in your community.

Key Takeaways:

- **Identify Key Demographics:** Understanding the diverse backgrounds and needs of your clients is the first step in tailoring your services effectively.
- **Analyze Psychographics:** As you research, go beyond demographic information and explore your clients' values, attitudes, and lifestyles. By understanding what drives your clients emotionally, you can create marketing messages that resonate on a personal level, making your firm more appealing and relatable.

- **Engage Adult Children:** When you build your marketing plan, it's important to recognize the critical role that adult children play in the decision-making process. Addressing their concerns alongside those of elderly clients can strengthen your firm's relationships and increase your appeal to this important demographic.

Addressing Client Concerns

Understanding your clients' demographics and psychographics is just the beginning of an effective marketing strategy. The next crucial step is addressing their concerns effectively.

Clients in elder law and estate planning often come to you with a bunch of worries, ranging from financial security to healthcare and legacy planning. How you handle these concerns can set your firm apart, build lasting trust, and establish you as a go-to resource for your clients.

Consider the primary concerns that hypothetical clients like John and Mary or Susan might have. The McDonalds, being financially stable, might be worried about protecting their assets from potential future healthcare costs. They may also be concerned about the tax implications of their estate and ensuring that their wealth is transferred smoothly to their heirs.

On the other hand, Susan might be more focused on qualifying for Medicaid and finding affordable long-term care options. Understanding these specific concerns allows you to tailor your communication strategies and meet their needs directly.

Empathy is a powerful tool when addressing client concerns. When clients feel that you genuinely understand their fears and are committed to helping them navigate these challenges, they're more likely to trust you and engage your services.

For example, when discussing Medicaid planning with a client like Susan, acknowledging the emotional stress and uncertainty she might be experiencing can make a significant impact. Simple, reassuring phrases like, "I understand how overwhelming this process can be, and I'm here to help you every step of the way," can provide comfort and build rapport. This empathetic approach is often what turns a hesitant inquiry into a loyal client relationship.

Another effective strategy is providing clear, actionable information that addresses common concerns. Many clients are unfamiliar with the intricacies of elder law and estate planning, which can make the process seem daunting. By breaking down complex legal concepts into simple, understandable terms, you can alleviate some of their anxiety.

This step can take many different forms in the world of marketing, such as a free client guide or a series of blog posts that explain the basics of Medicaid planning, estate taxes, or other high-value topics. You'll want to choose options that educate your clients and position your firm as a knowledgeable and trustworthy resource.

As you curate your strategy, anticipate the questions and worries your clients might have before they even ask. Being proactive in this area ultimately results in resonant, quality assets that build your client pool quickly..

For example: One of the firms we've worked with noticed that many clients were anxious about the impact of potential changes in legislation on their estate plans. To address this, they started a monthly newsletter that provided updates on relevant legislative changes and explained how these changes might affect their clients.

This proactive approach not only kept their clients informed but also demonstrated the firm's commitment to staying on top of industry developments and protecting their client's interests.

Lastly, don't underestimate the importance of follow-up in addressing client concerns. A simple phone call or email shows that you care about their well-being and are committed to providing ongoing support. This level of attention to detail can make a significant difference in building trust and strengthening your client relationships.

Addressing client concerns is a multifaceted process that requires empathy, clear communication, and proactive information sharing. By understanding and addressing the specific worries and needs of your clients, you can build trust, demonstrate your expertise, and, ultimately, grow your practice. Remember: Your goal is not just to provide legal services but to be a trusted advisor who helps clients navigate some of the most challenging and emotional aspects of their lives.

Key Takeaways:

- **Empathy is Key:** Approach every client interaction with empathy, understanding their unique fears and challenges.
- **Provide Clear, Actionable Information:** Break down complex legal concepts into simple terms to alleviate client anxiety and position your firm as a trusted resource.

- **Be Proactive in Your Approach:** Anticipate your clients' concerns and address them before they arise. This proactive approach showcases your commitment to their well-being and keeps them informed.

Crafting Personas

Personas, in this context, are semi-fictional representations of your ideal clients based on real data and insights about your existing client base. By crafting detailed personas, you gain a deeper understanding of your clients' needs, behaviors, and motivations, allowing you to tailor your marketing strategies to resonate more deeply with them.

To begin crafting personas, start by gathering data from various sources. You can find this information in:

- Client interviews
- Surveys
- Website analytics
- Feedback from your office team (or from your clients themselves)

Your goal throughout this process is to collect as much information as possible about your clients' demographics, psychographics, and behaviors. For example, you might discover that a significant portion of your clients are retired professionals aged 65-75 who are concerned about estate planning and long-term care.

Once you have gathered this data, the next step is to identify common patterns and group similar clients together. As you do this, you might identify names that define your grouped personas, such as "The Retired Professional," "The Caregiver," and "The Financially Insecure Senior".

Let's discuss each of these possible personas in more detail, as you'll likely find clients in your base that align with these definitions:

The Retired Professional: This persona represents clients like John and Mary, who are financially stable and have a clear vision for their estate planning. They are typically in their late 60s to early 70s, own their home, and have a diversified investment portfolio. Their primary concerns include protecting their assets from potential healthcare costs, minimizing estate taxes, and ensuring a smooth transfer of wealth to their heirs. They value expertise, professionalism, and personalized service.

The Caregiver: This persona represents the adult children of elderly clients, often in their 40s or 50s. They are juggling careers, families, and the responsibility of caring for their aging parents. Their primary concerns include finding affordable long-term care options, navigating Medicaid planning, and ensuring their parents' financial security. They value empathy, clear communication, and practical solutions that can alleviate their stress and burden.

The Financially Insecure Senior: This persona represents clients like Susan, who have limited financial resources and are worried about their future. They are typically in their mid-60s to early 70s, may be widowed or single, and have modest savings. Their primary concerns include qualifying for Medicaid, finding affordable healthcare, and securing their financial future. They value affordability, transparency, and compassionate guidance.

With these personas in mind, you can tailor your marketing messages and strategies to address the specific needs and concerns of each group.

Key Takeaways:

- **Develop Detailed Personas:** Crafting personas based on real data allows you to gain insights into your client's needs and behaviors. It also allows you to create targeted marketing strategies that resonate with specific client segments.

- **Tailor Your Marketing:** Use these personas to shape your content and outreach strategies.
- **Build Trust Through Understanding:** Show your clients that you understand their unique challenges by providing tailored solutions and compassionate guidance.

CHAPTER 2:
CRAFTING COMPELLING HEADLINES AND CALLS-TO-ACTION

The Psychology of Engagement

Understanding the psychology of engagement is crucial for crafting compelling headlines and calls-to-action (CTAs) that drive clicks and conversions. To do this well, you'll need a connection that motivates your audience to take action and an understanding of the psychological principles that influence human behavior.

The first thing to consider is attention. In a world where people are constantly bombarded with information, capturing and holding attention is more challenging than ever.

To capture someone's attention, your headlines must be clear, concise, and relevant to your audience's needs and interests. Use strong, action-oriented words and avoid jargon or overly complex language.

A generic headline like "Understanding Medicaid Planning" might not capture attention as effectively as a more specific and emotionally resonant headline like "How to Protect Your Assets and Qualify for Medicaid: A Step-by-Step Guide," for example.

The latter not only promises valuable information but also addresses a common concern among your target audience — making it more likely to capture their attention.

The second key principle to consider is emotional resonance. People are more likely to engage with content that evokes an emotional response.

You can leverage emotional resonance by addressing their fears, desires, and motivations. Ideally, you'll use emotional resonance at every client touchpoint in your process — especially in your headlines and CTAs. For example, a headline like "Secure Your Family's Future: Essential Estate Planning Tips" taps into the emotional desire to protect loved ones and ensure their well-being.

Social proof is another powerful psychological principle that can enhance engagement. People tend to trust and follow the actions of others, especially when they are uncertain. Firms can leverage this principle via case studies, published testimonials, and social shares that leverage their reach and impact.

Scarcity and urgency are also effective psychological triggers that can drive engagement. When people perceive that an opportunity is limited or time-sensitive, they are more likely to take action. CTAs, such as "Limited Spots Available for Our Free Estate Planning Workshop – Register Now" or "Don't Miss Out – Claim Your Free Consultation Today" reinforce this urgency and encourage immediate action.

Reciprocity also enhances engagement. When you offer something of value, people feel a sense of obligation to reciprocate. This can be as simple as providing valuable information, free resources, or personalized advice.

Understanding the psychology of engagement is essential for driving clicks and conversions. By leveraging principles such as attention, emotional resonance, social proof, scarcity, urgency, and reciprocity, you can create marketing messages that resonate with your audience and motivate them to take action.

Remember: The goal here is not just to capture attention but to create a meaningful connection that leads to engagement and, ultimately, client conversion.

Key Takeaways:

- **Capture Attention:** Use clear, concise, and relevant headlines that resonate with your audience and immediately grab their attention.
- **Evoke Emotional Responses:** Craft headlines and CTAs that resonate emotionally with your clients by addressing their fears, desires, and motivations.
- **Leverage Social Proof:** Highlight the positive experiences of others to build trust and encourage potential clients to take action.
- **Create Urgency:** Use scarcity and urgency to prompt immediate engagement, driving quicker responses to your offers.
- **Simplify and Personalize:** Ensure that your messages are clear, simple, and tailored to the specific needs of different client segments for maximum impact.

Headline Writing Techniques

Crafting effective, attention-grabbing headlines is both an art and a science. A well-written headline can be the difference between a potential client clicking on your content or scrolling past.

Here's a quick checklist to use as you begin to create your own, leaving you with the most effective and powerful headlines possible:

Be Clear and Specific

Clarity is paramount when writing headlines. As you craft your headline, your audience should immediately understand what the content is about and why it matters to them. Ambiguous or vague headlines can confuse readers and deter them from engaging.

For example, instead of a generic headline like "Estate Planning Tips," opt for something more specific, like: "5 Essential Estate Planning Tips to Protect Your Family's Future."

Use Numbers and Lists

Headlines that include numbers and lists tend to perform well because they promise concise, digestible information. For instance, a headline like "7 Common Mistakes in Medicaid Planning and How to Avoid Them" is likely to attract more attention than a more general headline.

Address Pain Points

Effective headlines often address the specific pain points or concerns of your audience. By acknowledging their challenges, you create a sense of empathy and urgency.

For example, a headline like "Worried About Long-Term Care Costs? Discover Affordable Solutions" directly addresses a common concern among elderly clients and their families.

Highlight Benefits

Your headlines should clearly convey the benefits of engaging with your content. If you're not sure where to start, consider asking yourself: *"What do I want the reader to gain from clicking on my link?"*

Use Power Words

Power words are emotionally charged words that can evoke strong reactions and drive engagement. Words like "essential," "proven," "ultimate," "secret," and "exclusive" can add a sense of importance and urgency to your headlines.

Ask Questions

Questions can be an effective way to engage your audience by tapping into their curiosity and encouraging them to seek answers. A well-crafted question can also make your content feel more interactive and personalized. For example, a headline like "Are You Prepared for the Financial Impact of Aging?" prompts the reader to reflect on their own situation and consider the value of your content.

Create a Sense of Urgency

Urgency can be a powerful motivator for engagement. By suggesting that the information is time-sensitive or that the opportunity is limited, you can prompt readers to take immediate action. This technique can be particularly effective for promoting events, special offers, or time-sensitive content.

Use Emotional Triggers

Emotional triggers can make your headlines more compelling by appealing to the reader's feelings and desires. Whether it's fear, hope, curiosity, or excitement, tapping into emotions can drive engagement.

Incorporate Keywords

Incorporating relevant keywords into your headlines can improve your content's visibility in search engine results and attract more organic traffic. However, keywords should be naturally integrated into the headline without compromising clarity or readability.

For example, a headline like "Medicaid Planning for Seniors: A Comprehensive Guide" includes the keyword "Medicaid planning" while clearly conveying the topic and target audience.

This technique helps to optimize your content for search engines while maintaining its appeal to readers.

Test and Iterate

It's important to test different headline variations to determine what resonates best with your audience. You can do this using A/B testing. For example, you might test two versions of a headline: "5 Essential Estate Planning Tips" versus "5 Estate Planning Tips to Protect Your Family's Future," refining your headline writing techniques as you receive your findings.

Mastering headline writing techniques is key to driving engagement in the competitive field of elder law and estate planning. By using the techniques outlined in this section, you can craft compelling headlines that resonate with your audience and motivate them to take action.

Key Takeaways:

- **Be Clear and Specific:** Ensure your headlines are clear and specific, immediately conveying the value of your content.
- **Use Numbers and Lists:** Numbers can make your content more digestible and structured, increasing its appeal.

- **Address Pain Points:** Directly address the challenges your audience faces to capture their attention and show empathy.
- **Highlight Benefits:** Clearly state the benefits of engaging with your content to motivate readers to take action.
- **Incorporate Keywords:** Use relevant keywords naturally to improve SEO while maintaining clarity and appeal.
- **Test and Iterate:** Continuously test and refine your headlines to discover what resonates most with your audience.

Crafting Effective Calls-To-Action

Strong CTAs are critical for elder law and estate planning firms. A well-designed CTA serves as a bridge between your content and your audience's next step, guiding potential clients toward taking action — whether that's scheduling a consultation, signing up for a newsletter, or downloading a valuable resource.

Before you create CTAs that resonate and convert, it's essential that you understand the psychology behind client behavior. Clients often approach legal services with a mix of apprehension and urgency. They may be facing significant life changes, such as aging, health concerns, or the loss of a loved one. This emotional backdrop means that your CTAs must not only be persuasive but also empathetic — addressing the specific needs and concerns of your audience.

Understanding Client Needs

Before crafting your CTAs, take a moment to reflect on the unique challenges your clients face. For instance: An elderly client may be overwhelmed by the complexities of estate planning and may need reassurance that your firm can simplify the process. A CTA that emphasizes ease and support, such as "Schedule Your Free Consultation Today — Let Us Guide You Through the Process," speaks directly to that need.

Using Action-Oriented Language

Action-oriented verbs are an important part of your CTA, as they create a sense of urgency in your offer. Phrases like "Get Started," "Join Us," or "Claim Your Free Consultation" prompt users to take action rather than simply passively consume content.

Designing for Visibility

A well-placed, visually appealing CTA can significantly impact conversion rates. While this can look different on every asset, I recommend using contrasting colors to make your CTA stand out against the background of your website or marketing materials.

The button itself should be large enough to be easily clickable, especially on mobile devices where many users will interact with your content.

Consider the placement of your CTAs. They should be strategically positioned within your content, appearing at natural stopping points where readers are likely to be engaged.

An example of this would include placing a CTA at the end of a blog post summarizing key estate planning tips to capitalize on the reader's interest and prompt them to take the next step.

Testing and Iteration

Creating effective CTAs is not a one-time effort; it requires ongoing testing and refinement. A/B testing here, just as you would with your headlines, allows you to compare different versions of your CTAs to see which performs better.

If you're not sure where to start, consider experimenting with variations in wording, design, placement, and even the time of day you publish your content.

Crafting effective calls-to-action is a critical component of your marketing strategy. By understanding your audience's needs, using action-oriented language, designing for visibility, and committing to ongoing testing and iteration, you can create CTAs that capture attention and drive meaningful client engagement.

Key Takeaways

- **Tailor CTAs to Client Needs:** Understand the emotional and practical challenges your clients face and craft CTAs that address these concerns directly.
- **Use Action-Oriented Language:** Employ strong, action-driven verbs and create a sense of urgency to encourage immediate engagement.
- **Test and Refine:** Continuously A/B test your CTAs to identify what resonates best with your audience, allowing for ongoing improvement in your marketing efforts.

CHAPTER 3:
VISUAL CONTENT AND USER EXPERIENCE

The Power of Visual Storytelling

In an era where attention spans are shorter than ever, the ability to communicate complex information quickly and effectively is crucial for elder law and estate planning firms.

Visual content — such as images, infographics, videos, and more — has emerged as a powerful tool for storytelling, enabling firms to communicate their messages in a way that resonates with clients on an emotional level.

Visual storytelling is not just about making your content aesthetically pleasing; it's about enhancing understanding and retention. Research shows that people process visuals thousands of times faster than text, which means incorporating visual elements can significantly improve how your audience engages with your content.

Additionally, in industries where the subject matter can often be sensitive and complex (such as elder law), using visuals can help demystify legal processes and make them more approachable.

Creating Engaging Infographics

Infographics are particularly effective in breaking down intricate topics such as estate planning, elder law rights, or the probate process. By distilling information into bite-sized, visually appealing graphics, you can guide potential clients through the steps they need to take without overwhelming them.

When designing infographics, focus on clarity and simplicity. Use a clean layout, a limited color palette that aligns with your brand, and clear, concise text.

Leveraging Video Content

Video content is another powerful medium for storytelling. It allows you to convey emotion and personality in a way that text alone cannot. For elder law firms, videos can humanize your practice, showcasing your attorneys' expertise while also building trust with potential clients. Consider creating introductory videos that explain your services, client testimonials that share positive experiences, or educational videos that address common questions about estate planning.

When producing video content, authenticity is key. Clients want to see the real people behind the firm, so encourage your attorneys to share their personal stories or insights about why they chose to practice elder law. This approach not only fosters connection but also positions your firm as approachable and empathetic—qualities that are essential in a field where clients are often navigating challenging life transitions.

Incorporating Visuals into Your Website

Your website serves as the digital face of your firm, making it essential to integrate visual content effectively. As you do this, it's best to use high-quality images that reflect your firm's values and mission; and ensure that your website layout is clean and intuitive.

The Role of User Experience (UX)

Strong visual content should be complemented by a strong user experience. UX encompasses all aspects of the end-user's interaction with your firm's website, from navigation to accessibility. A seamless user experience ensures that potential clients can easily find the information they need and take the desired actions, such as filling out a contact form or scheduling a consultation.

To enhance UX, start by evaluating your website's navigation. *Is it intuitive? Are key pages easily accessible?*

Conduct user testing to gather feedback on how real clients interact with your site.

Mobile Optimization

As you optimize your design for mobile use, consider implementing a responsive design or site template. This means that your website should automatically adjust its layout and content based on the device being used.

Prior to launch, I recommend testing your site on various devices to ensure that all visual elements display correctly and that navigation remains smooth and free of lag from slow-loading pages.

Mobile-optimized content should be concise and scannable, made with short paragraphs and bullet points to enhance readability. Additionally, mobile users often skim content, so using headings and subheadings to break up text can help them quickly locate the information they need. Loading speed is a critical factor in mobile optimization. To enhance loading speed, consider the following strategies:

Optimize Images: You can do this by compressing images to reduce file size without sacrificing quality. Use formats like JPEG for photographs and PNG for graphics with transparency included.

Minimize HTTP Requests: Reduce the number of elements on your page (such as scripts and stylesheets) to decrease loading times.

Leverage Browser Caching: Enable browser caching to store certain elements of your website on users' devices, allowing for faster loading on subsequent visits.

Testing and Monitoring Mobile Performance

To ensure that your mobile optimization efforts are effective, regular testing and monitoring are essential. Use tools like Google's Mobile-Friendly Test to evaluate how well your website performs on mobile devices. This tool provides insights into potential issues and suggestions for improvement.

Additionally, I recommend that you monitor user behavior through paid and free analytics tools. Pay attention to metrics such as bounce rates, average session duration, and conversion rates for mobile users. If you notice discrepancies between mobile and desktop performance, it may indicate areas that require further optimization.

Real-World Example: A Case Study

Consider this example of a small elder law firm that recognized the need to enhance its online presence. The firm invested in a website redesign that prioritized visual storytelling and user experience. They incorporated infographics to explain the estate planning process and created a series of short videos featuring their attorneys discussing common legal concerns.

As a result of these changes, the firm saw a 50% increase in website traffic and a notable uptick in consultation requests. Clients reported feeling more informed and comfortable reaching out, thanks to the engaging and approachable content.

Key Takeaways

- **Utilize Visual Storytelling:** Incorporate infographics and videos to simplify complex legal topics and enhance client engagement.
- **Prioritize User Experience:** Ensure your website is intuitive and easy to navigate, addressing potential pain points for users.
- **Optimize for Mobile:** Implement responsive design to provide a seamless experience across all devices, catering to the growing number of mobile users.

Designing for Trust

Trust is key to quality firm assets. Your firm's website and visual content should be designed to convey professionalism, reliability, and empathy foremost, as this will be the first impression potential clients will have of your practice.

There are many factors that go into trustworthy design:

Professionalism
A well-designed website reflects the quality of your services. If your site appears outdated, cluttered, or unprofessional, it can lead potential clients to question your expertise and credibility. A clean, modern design signals that your firm is current and attentive to detail.

Investing in professional web design is not merely an aesthetic choice; it's a strategic decision that can significantly impact your firm's reputation.

As you design, consider the use of color psychology in your design choices. Colors evoke emotions and can influence perceptions. For example, blue is often associated with trust and reliability, making it a popular choice for legal websites. Green can convey a sense of calm and reassurance, which is particularly relevant in elder law.

By thoughtfully selecting your color palette, you can enhance the emotional connection clients feel with your firm.

Brand Identity

Your website should reflect a cohesive brand identity that aligns with your firm's values and mission. This includes consistent use of logos, fonts, and imagery across all platforms. A strong brand identity fosters recognition and trust, making clients more likely to engage with your content and services.

Testimonials and Case Studies

Incorporating client testimonials and case studies into your website design can further enhance trust, as they serve as an authentic endorsement of your services.

Accessibility

It's important that your website is accessible to all users, including those with disabilities. An accessible website not only expands your reach, but also demonstrates your firm's commitment to inclusivity and client care.

Implementing accessibility features, such as alt text for images, keyboard navigation, and screen reader compatibility, ensures that all potential clients can engage with your content.

Accessibility also extends to the readability of your site's text. To put this into practice, use clear, legible fonts and maintain a good contrast between text and background colors. Also consider breaking up large blocks of text with headings, bullet points, and visuals to make your content more digestible.

A well-organized layout enhances user experience and reinforces the impression of professionalism.

Designing for trust is a critical aspect of creating a successful online presence for elder law and estate planning firms. By prioritizing professional design, cohesive branding, client testimonials, accessibility, and readability, you'll foster a sense of trust and reliability that resonates with potential clients.

Key Takeaways

- **Invest in Professional Design:** A well-designed website reflects the quality of your services and establishes credibility with potential clients.
- **Create a Cohesive Brand Identity:** Consistent use of logos, colors, and imagery fosters recognition and trust, making clients more likely to engage.
- **Incorporate Testimonials and Case Studies:** Positive reviews and detailed case studies build credibility and reassure potential clients of your firm's expertise.

Optimizing for Conversion

A visually appealing site can draw visitors in, but it's the strategic design elements and user experience that ultimately guide them toward taking action or "converting" — whether that's scheduling a consultation, registering for a workshop, signing up for a newsletter, or downloading valuable resources.

Understanding the Conversion Funnel

To optimize for conversion, we first have to explore and understand the conversion funnel, which represents the journey potential clients take from awareness to action.

This funnel typically consists of several stages: awareness, interest, consideration, and action. Each stage requires different strategies to effectively guide users toward the final conversion.

At the **awareness** stage, potential clients discover your firm through various channels: such as search engines, social media, or referrals. Here, your website or other channels should capture their interest with compelling visuals and engaging content that addresses their needs.

As users move to the **interest** stage, they begin to evaluate their options. This is where your website's design and content must work together to provide clear information about your services.

Here, consider using visuals (such as infographics or videos) to explain complex legal concepts in an accessible way. You can also highlight your firm's unique value proposition and the benefits of choosing your services over competitors.

In the **consideration** stage, potential clients are weighing their options and may be looking for reassurance. This is an excellent opportunity to showcase client testimonials, case studies, and success stories that demonstrate your firm's expertise and positive outcomes. By providing social proof, you can alleviate concerns and build trust.

Finally, at the **action** stage, your goal is to prompt users to take the desired action. This is where effective calls-to-action (CTAs) come into play, guiding users toward scheduling a consultation or filling out a contact form.

Designing Effective CTAs

Effective CTAs are critical for conversion optimization. They should be clear, compelling, and strategically placed throughout your website. Typically, this means that they'll remain visible without requiring users to scroll excessively.

As you craft your CTA, use action-oriented language that encourages users to take the next step, such as "Schedule Your Free Consultation Today" or "Download Our Estate Planning Checklist."

Streamlining the User Journey

A streamlined user journey is essential for conversion optimization. Different methods of streamlining and simplifying include:

- Minimizing friction points that could deter potential clients from taking action.
- Evaluating your website's navigation to ensure it's intuitive and user-friendly.
- Optimizing your menu structure so users can easily engage with your services.
- Optimizing your forms to be simple and straightforward, avoiding excessive information gathering upfront.

Utilizing Analytics for Continuous Improvement

Leveraging analytics tools is a key step when it comes to optimizing for conversion.

Tools like Google Analytics can provide valuable insights into how visitors interact with your site, including which pages they visit, how long they stay, and where they drop off in the conversion process. Analysis of this data can help you to identify areas for improvement.

Key Takeaways

- **Understand the Conversion Funnel:** Tailor your website content and design to guide potential clients through the stages of awareness, interest, consideration, and action.
- **Design Effective CTAs:** Use clear, compelling language and strategic placement to encourage users to take action, ensuring CTAs stand out visually.
- **Streamline the User Journey:** Minimize friction points by creating intuitive navigation and simple contact forms, enhancing the overall user experience.

CHAPTER 4:
SEO AND LOCAL SEARCH OPTIMIZATION

Understanding SEO Basics

Having a strong online presence is crucial for elder law and estate planning firms. Search Engine Optimization, or SEO, is how you start putting yourself in front of your ideal clientele.

The Importance of Keywords

Specific words or phrases — keywords — that users enter into search engines are the heart and soul of SEO. Choose carefully, opting for options that both reflect the services you offer and the concerns of your target audience.

The first step to choosing the right keywords is to research which ones are the best fit for your target audience. Tools like Google Keyword Planner, SEMrush, or Ahrefs can help you identify relevant keywords with high search volumes. (For example, terms like "estate planning attorney," "elder law services," or "wills and trusts" are likely to be valuable for your practice).

Once you have a list of keywords, strategically incorporate them into your website content. This includes your homepage, service pages, blog posts, and meta descriptions.

As you do this, note that natural keyword usage is better than forced. Forcing keywords in for ranking (a practice known as "keyword stuffing") can lead to penalties from search engines, ultimately diminishing the quality of your content.

On-Page SEO Elements

On-page SEO refers to the optimization of individual web pages to rank higher and earn more relevant traffic. Key elements of on-page SEO include:

Title Tags: The title tag is one of the most important on-page SEO elements. It should include your primary keyword and accurately describe the content of the page. Keep it under 60 characters to ensure it displays fully in search results.

Meta Descriptions: A meta description is a brief summary of a web page that appears in search results. While it doesn't directly influence rankings, a compelling meta description can improve click-through rates. Aim for 150-160 characters and include relevant keywords.

Header Tags: Use header tags (or H1, H2, and H3 tags) to structure your content. The H1 tag should contain your primary keyword and clearly indicate the topic of the page. Subheadings (known as the H2 and H3 headings) can help organize your content and make it more scannable for readers.

Image Alt Text: Images can enhance your content, but search engines cannot interpret them without proper descriptions. Use alt text to describe your images, incorporating relevant keywords where appropriate.

Internal Linking: Internal links connect different pages on your website, helping users navigate and discover related content. They also signal to search engines the importance of certain pages. (For example, linking from a blog post about estate planning to your service page can improve visibility).

Off-Page SEO Factors

While on-page SEO focuses on your website, off-page SEO refers to external factors that influence your site's authority and ranking. One of the most significant off-page SEO elements is backlinks — or links from other websites to your content.

High-quality backlinks from reputable sources signal to search engines that your content is valuable and trustworthy.

To build backlinks, consider guest blogging on reputable legal websites, collaborating with local organizations, or participating in community events. Each of these activities can help you earn links back to your site, improving your authority and search rankings.

The Role of Content in SEO

Content is a cornerstone of effective SEO. Creating high-quality, informative content not only helps you rank for relevant keywords; it also establishes your firm as an authority in elder law and estate planning. Regularly publishing blog posts, articles, or guides can attract visitors to your site and encourage them to engage with your services.

When creating content, focus on addressing the questions and concerns of your target audience. Additionally, consider using various content formats, such as videos, infographics, and podcasts, to reach a broader audience.

Real-World Example: An SEO Success Story

Let's look at a case study of a small elder law firm that successfully improved its online visibility through SEO.

Initially, the firm struggled to attract clients through its website, as it ranked low in search results. They decided to invest in an SEO strategy that included keyword research, on-page optimization, and content creation.

The firm identified relevant keywords and optimized its website accordingly, updating title tags, meta descriptions, and header tags. They also began publishing regular blog posts addressing common client concerns, such as "How to Choose the Right Power of Attorney," and "Understanding Medicaid Planning."

Within six months, the firm saw a 150% increase in organic traffic and a significant rise in consultation requests. By implementing a comprehensive SEO strategy, they established themselves as a go-to resource for elder law services in their community.

Understanding the basics of SEO is essential for elder law and estate planning firms looking to enhance their online presence. By focusing on keyword research, on-page and off-page optimization, and high-quality content creation, your firm can improve its visibility in search engine results and attract more potential clients.

Key Takeaways

- **Conduct Keyword Research:** Identify relevant keywords that potential clients are searching for and incorporate them naturally into your website content.
- **Optimize On-Page Elements:** Focus on title tags, meta descriptions, header tags, and image alt text to improve your website's SEO performance.
- **Create High-Quality Content:** Regularly publish informative and engaging content that addresses client concerns, establishing your firm as an authority in elder law and estate planning.

Local SEO Strategies

Most clients seeking legal services prefer to work with firms that are geographically close to them. Local SEO helps ensure that your firm appears in search results when potential clients search for legal services in your area.

Claiming and Optimizing Your Google Business Profile Listing

One of the most effective ways to enhance your local SEO is by claiming and optimizing your Google Business Profile (GBP) listing.

GBP is a free tool that allows businesses to manage their online presence across Google, including search and maps. When potential clients search for elder law or estate planning services in your area, your GBP listing can appear prominently in local search results.

To optimize your GBP listing, start by ensuring that all information is accurate and up to date. This includes your firm's name, address, phone number, and website URL. Note that the information on your GBP listing should match what is displayed on your website and other online directories.

Additionally, I also recommend taking advantage of the other features GBP offers. You can use GBP to upload high-quality images of your office, team, and events to give potential clients a glimpse of your practice. Or, you can encourage satisfied clients to leave positive reviews on your GBP listing, as these reviews can significantly influence potential clients' decisions.

Remember: Social proof and trust is a two-way street. Responding to reviews — both positive and negative — demonstrates your commitment to client satisfaction and can further enhance your firm's reputation.

Local Keywords and Content Creation

Incorporating local keywords into your website content is another essential strategy for local SEO. Local keywords typically include your city or region along with relevant legal terms.

For example, Instead of just targeting "estate planning attorney," consider phrases like "estate planning attorney in [Your City]" or "elder law services in [Your Region]."

Creating localized content can also help establish your firm as a trusted resource in your community. Consider writing articles or blog posts that address local laws, regulations, or events related to elder law and estate planning. This not only improves your local SEO; it also demonstrates your expertise and commitment to serving your (local) community.

Building Local Citations

Local citations are online mentions of your business's name, address, and phone number (or NAP) on various websites and directories. Building local citations is crucial for improving your local SEO, as search engines use these citations to verify your firm's legitimacy and relevance in your area.

I recommend starting by ensuring that your NAP information is consistent across all online platforms, including your website, social media profiles, and local directories. Common directories to consider as you take this step include Yelp, Yellow Pages, and local bar association directories.

Additionally, I recommend seeking out industry-specific directories that cater to legal services. Being listed in reputable directories can enhance your firm's visibility and authority, making it easier for potential clients to find you.

Engaging with the Local Community

Engaging with your local community can also boost your local SEO efforts. Participating in community events, sponsoring local organizations, or hosting educational seminars can increase your firm's visibility and create opportunities for backlinks to your website.

Real-World Example: A Local SEO Success Story

Let's examine a case study of a small elder law firm that successfully implemented local SEO strategies to increase its visibility. Initially, the firm struggled to attract clients, as it was not appearing in local search results. They decided to focus on optimizing their online presence for local SEO.

The firm began by claiming and optimizing their GBP listing, ensuring that all information was accurate and up to date. They also encouraged satisfied clients to leave positive reviews and actively responded to all feedback.

Next, they conducted keyword research to identify relevant local keywords and incorporated these into their website content. They published blog posts addressing local estate planning laws and created resources tailored to residents of their city.

Finally, the firm built local citations by listing their practice in various online directories and engaging with the community through local events.

As a result of these efforts, the firm saw a 200% increase in local search visibility within six months. They began receiving more inquiries from potential clients, leading to a significant increase in consultation requests.

This case highlights the fact that effective local SEO strategies are essential for elder law and estate planning firms looking to enhance their online presence and attract clients in their area.

Key Takeaways

- **Optimize Your Google Business Profile Listing:** Claim and enhance your GBP listing with accurate information, high-quality images, and positive client reviews to improve local visibility.

- **Incorporate Local Keywords:** Use local keywords in your website content to attract potential clients searching for legal services in your area.
- **Build Local Citations:** Ensure consistent NAP information across online directories and engage with your local community to enhance your firm's authority and visibility.

Google Business Profile Optimization

Google Business Profile (GBP) is an indispensable tool for elder law and estate planning firms looking to enhance their local SEO efforts. By optimizing your GBP profile, you can significantly increase your visibility in local search results, making it easier for potential clients to find and connect with your firm.

This section will talk about the key strategies for effectively optimizing your GBP listing.

Claiming Your GBP Listing

The first step in optimizing your GBP profile is to claim your listing. If you haven't already done so, visit the Google Business Profile website and follow the prompts to verify your business.

Verification typically involves receiving a postcard from Google with a verification code sent to your business address. Once verified, you gain control over the information displayed about your firm.

Completing Your Profile

A complete GBP profile is crucial for attracting potential clients. A comprehensively complete profile includes:

Your Business Name: Use your firm's official name as it appears in the real world. Avoid adding keywords or phrases that could mislead users.

Address: Provide your complete business address. This is essential for local SEO, as it helps Google determine your firm's location and relevance to local searches.

Phone Number: Include a local phone number that clients can easily reach.

Website URL: Link to your firm's website to direct traffic and provide more information about your services.

Business Hours: Clearly state your operating hours. If your hours vary on holidays or special occasions, be sure to update this information accordingly.

Categories: Choose relevant categories that accurately describe your services. For elder law and estate planning, categories might include "Elder Law Attorney," "Estate Planning Attorney," or "Law Firm."

Selecting the right categories helps Google match your firm with relevant searches.

Services: List the specific services your firm offers, such as "Wills and Trusts," "Probate Assistance," or "Medicaid Planning." Providing detailed descriptions of your services can help potential clients understand what you offer.

Adding Visual Content

Visual content plays a significant role in attracting potential clients to your GBP listing. High-quality images can showcase your firm's personality and professionalism. As you optimize your profile, consider including:

Office Photos: Images of your office space can help potential clients feel more comfortable and familiar with your firm before they visit.

Team Photos: Showcasing your attorneys and staff humanizes your practice and builds trust. Consider including professional headshots and candid photos of your team in action.

Event Photos: If your firm participates in community events or hosts educational seminars, share photos from these activities. This demonstrates your firm's engagement with the community and can attract local clients.

Encouraging Client Reviews

Client reviews are a critical component of your GBP profile. Positive reviews not only enhance your firm's credibility — they also influence potential clients' decisions. Encourage satisfied clients to leave reviews on your GBP listing by:

Asking Directly: After a successful consultation, seminar, or service, kindly ask clients if they would be willing to leave a review. You can provide them with a direct link to your GBP listing for convenience.

Sending Follow-Up Emails: After a consultation, send a follow-up email thanking clients for their business and inviting them to share their experience through a review.

Responding to Reviews: Engage with clients by responding to their reviews, whether positive or negative. Thanking clients for positive feedback shows appreciation while addressing negative reviews demonstrates your commitment to resolving issues and improving client satisfaction.

Posts and Updates

GBP allows you to share posts and updates directly on your profile. This feature can be used to promote upcoming events, share helpful articles, or announce new services.

Regularly updating your GBP profile with fresh content can keep potential clients engaged and informed.

As such, consider creating posts that highlight:

Educational Content: Share links to blog posts or articles that address common questions or concerns related to elder law and estate planning.

Community Involvement: Post about your firm's participation in local events, sponsorships, or volunteer activities.

Special Offers: Use GBP posts to inform potential clients if your firm is running a promotion or offering a free consultation,

Monitoring Insights and Performance

GBP provides valuable insights that can help you understand how potential clients are interacting with your profile. Regularly monitor these insights to track metrics such as:

Search Queries: See what search terms clients are using to find your firm. This information can help you refine your SEO strategy and identify new keywords to target.

Client Actions: Track how clients are engaging with your listing, including how many are calling your firm, visiting your website, or requesting directions.

Photo Views: Monitor how often your photos are viewed compared to competitors. This can help you assess the effectiveness of your visual content.

By analyzing these insights, you can make informed decisions to enhance your GBP profile and improve your local SEO strategy.

Real-World Example: A GBP Optimization Success Story

Consider the case of a small elder law firm that struggled to attract clients through online searches. After realizing the importance of Google Business Profile, they decided to optimize their GBP profile.

They claimed their listing and ensured that all information was accurate and complete. The firm added high-quality images of their office and team, encouraging clients to leave reviews. They also began posting regular updates about community events and educational seminars.

Within a few months, the firm saw a significant increase in inquiries from potential clients. Their GBP listing appeared prominently in local search results, leading to a 35% increase in consultation requests.

Optimizing your Google Business Profile listing is a critical component of your local SEO strategy. By claiming your listing, completing your profile, adding visual content, encouraging client reviews, utilizing posts, and monitoring insights, you can enhance your firm's visibility in local search results and attract more potential clients.

Key Takeaways

- **Claim and Complete Your GBP Listing:** Ensure all information is accurate and comprehensive, including your business name, address, phone number, and services.
- **Add Visual Content:** Use high-quality images of your office, team, and community involvement to enhance your GBP profile and attract potential clients.
- **Encourage Client Reviews:** Actively seek reviews from satisfied clients and engage with feedback to build credibility and trust in your firm.

Tracking SEO Performance

Tracking the performance of your SEO efforts is essential for understanding what strategies are working and where improvements can be made.

This section will explore the key metrics to track, the tools available for monitoring, and how to use this data to enhance your SEO strategy.

Key Metrics to Monitor

Organic Traffic: One of the most fundamental metrics to track is the amount of organic traffic your website receives. Visitors who arrive at your site through unpaid search results constitute organic traffic. You can use tools like Google Analytics to monitor this metric over time and identify trends.

Keyword Rankings: Tracking the rankings of your targeted keywords is crucial for assessing the effectiveness of your SEO strategy. Tools like SEMrush, Ahrefs, or Moz can help you monitor how your keywords are performing in search engine results pages (SERPs).

Click-Through Rate (CTR): The CTR measures the percentage of users who click on your website link after seeing it in search results. A higher CTR indicates that your title tags and meta descriptions are compelling and relevant to users' search queries. If your CTR is low, consider revising your title tags and meta descriptions to make them more engaging.

Bounce Rate: The bounce rate represents the percentage of visitors who leave your site after viewing only one page. A high bounce rate may indicate that users are not finding the information they expected or that your content is not engaging enough. As you create content, I recommend analyzing your pages with high bounce rates to identify potential issues and make necessary adjustments.

Conversion Rate: Ultimately, the goal of your SEO efforts is to convert visitors into clients. Tracking the conversion rate — whether that's scheduling a consultation, signing up for a newsletter, or downloading a resource — will help you assess the effectiveness of your website in turning traffic into actionable leads. Use Google Analytics to set up goals and track conversions.

Tools for Tracking SEO Performance

Several tools can assist you in monitoring your SEO performance effectively:

Google Analytics: This free tool provides comprehensive insights into your website traffic, user behavior, and conversion metrics. You can track organic traffic, bounce rates, and conversion rates, allowing you to make more strategic marketing decisions.

Google Search Console: This tool helps you monitor your website's presence in Google search results. It provides valuable information about keyword rankings, click-through rates, and any issues that may affect your site's performance, such as crawl errors or mobile usability problems.

SEMrush or Ahrefs: These paid tools offer advanced SEO analytics, including keyword tracking, backlink analysis, and competitor insights. They can help you identify opportunities for improvement and track your progress over time.

Moz: Moz provides a suite of SEO tools, including keyword tracking, site audits, and local SEO insights. Their user-friendly interface makes it easy to monitor your SEO performance and identify areas for optimization.

Using Data to Refine Your SEO Strategy

Tracking SEO performance is not just about collecting data; it's about using that data to inform your strategy. As such, I always recommend that my clients regularly review their metrics to identify trends and patterns.

For example, if you notice that certain blog posts are driving significant organic traffic, consider creating additional content on similar topics to capitalize on that interest.

A/B testing is a valuable strategy for refining your SEO efforts. Consider experimenting with different title tags, meta descriptions, or content formats to see which variations yield better results. By continuously testing and iterating, you can optimize your website for maximum performance.

Real-World Example: An SEO Tracking Success Story

Let's look at a case study of an elder law firm that implemented a robust SEO tracking strategy to enhance its online presence. Initially, the firm struggled to attract clients through organic search, and they realized they needed to monitor their performance closely.

They set up Google Analytics and Google Search Console to track key metrics such as organic traffic, keyword rankings, and conversion rates. By analyzing this data, they identified that certain blog posts about Medicaid planning were driving significant traffic but had low conversion rates.

In response, the firm optimized these blog posts by adding clear calls-to-action and links to their consultation scheduling page. They also created additional content around related topics, such as "Understanding Medicaid Eligibility" and "Common Medicaid Myths."

As a result of these efforts, the firm saw a massive increase in organic traffic over six months and a 50%+ increase in consultation requests.

Tracking SEO performance is essential for elder law and estate planning firms looking to enhance their online presence and attract clients. By monitoring key metrics, utilizing effective tools, and using data to refine your strategy, you can optimize your SEO efforts and drive meaningful results for your practice.

Key Takeaways

- **Monitor Key Metrics:** Track organic traffic, keyword rankings, click-through rates, bounce rates, and conversion rates to assess the effectiveness of your SEO strategy.
- **Utilize SEO Tools:** Leverage tools like Google Analytics, Google Search Console, SEMrush, or Ahrefs to gain insights into your website's performance and identify areas for improvement.
- **Refine Your Strategy with Data:** Regularly analyze your metrics to identify trends and make data-driven decisions to optimize your content and improve conversion rates.

CHAPTER 5:
MEASURING AND IMPROVING CONTENT PERFORMANCE

Key Metrics to Track

Measuring content performance is essential for understanding what resonates with your audience and driving meaningful engagement. By tracking the right metrics, such as the ones listed below, you can gain insights into how well your content is performing, identify areas for improvement, and refine your content strategy to meet the needs of your clients better.

Traffic Metrics

Traffic metrics provide a foundational understanding of how many people are visiting your content. Key traffic metrics to monitor include:

Page Views: This metric indicates how many times a specific page on your website has been viewed. High page views can suggest that your content is attracting interest, but it's essential to analyze this metric in conjunction with other metrics to gauge true engagement.

Unique Visitors: This metric counts the number of distinct individuals visiting your site over a specific period. Tracking unique visitors helps you understand your audience size and whether your content is reaching new clients.

Traffic Sources: Understanding where your traffic is coming from helps you identify which channels are most effective for your content distribution, resulting in more efficiently allocated resources.

Engagement Metrics

Engagement metrics provide deeper insights into how users interact with your content. Key engagement metrics to track include:

Average Time on Page: This metric indicates how long visitors spend on a particular page. A longer average time suggests that users find your content valuable and engaging.

Bounce Rate: The bounce rate measures the percentage of visitors who leave your site after viewing only one page. A high bounce rate may suggest that users are not finding what they are looking for, prompting a need for content optimization or improved navigation.

Pages per Session: This metric tracks the average number of pages a user visits during a single session on your site. A higher number of pages per session indicates that users are engaged and exploring your content further.

Conversion Metrics

Ultimately, the goal of your content is to drive conversions — whether that's scheduling a consultation, signing up for a newsletter, or downloading a resource.

Key conversion metrics to monitor include:

Conversion Rate: This metric measures the percentage of visitors who complete a desired action on your site. For example, If 100 visitors land on a page and 10 schedule a consultation, the conversion rate for that page is 10%.

Goal Completions: In Google Analytics, you can set up specific goals to track actions you want users to take, such as filling out a contact form or downloading a guide. Monitoring goal completions provides insight into how well your content is facilitating these actions.

Lead Generation: For elder law and estate planning firms, lead generation is a critical metric. Consider tracking the number of leads generated from specific content pieces, such as blog posts or downloadable resources, to understand which content is most effective in attracting potential clients.

Social Media Metrics

If you're sharing your content on social media, tracking social media metrics can provide valuable insights into how your content is performing across different platforms. Key social media metrics to monitor include:

Shares and Likes: The number of shares and likes your content receives indicates how well it resonates with your audience. High engagement on social media can amplify your reach and attract new visitors to your website.

Comments and Interactions: Monitoring comments and interactions on your social media posts can provide qualitative insights into how your audience perceives your content. Engaging with users in the comments can also foster community and build relationships.

Tracking key metrics is essential for understanding the effectiveness of your content and refining your strategy. By focusing on traffic, engagement, conversion, and social media metrics, elder law and estate planning firms can gain valuable insights that drive meaningful results.

Key Takeaways

- **Monitor Traffic Metrics:** Track page views, unique visitors, and traffic sources to understand how many people are engaging with your content and where they are coming from.
- **Analyze Engagement Metrics:** Measure average time on page, bounce rate, and pages per session to assess how users interact with your content and identify areas for improvement.
- **Focus on Conversion Metrics:** Monitor conversion rates, goal completions, and lead generation to evaluate the effectiveness of your content in driving desired actions and attracting potential clients.

Using Analytics Tools

Leveraging analytics tools is essential for firms looking to measure and improve content performance. In this section, we will explore some of the most effective analytics tools available and how to use them to enhance your content strategy.

Google Analytics

Google Analytics is one of the most widely used analytics tools, offering a comprehensive suite of features to track website performance. Here are some key functionalities that can help you measure content performance:

Audience Insights: Google Analytics provides demographic information about your website visitors, including age, gender, and location. Understanding your audience can help you tailor your content to better meet their needs.

Behavior Flow: This feature visualizes the path users take through your website, showing how they navigate from one page to another. Analyzing the behavior flow can help you identify which content keeps users engaged and where they drop off.

Content Performance Reports: Google Analytics allows you to track the performance of individual pages, including metrics such as page views, average time on page, and bounce rate. You can use these reports to identify high-performing content and areas that may need improvement.

Goal Tracking: Set up specific goals in Google Analytics to track conversions, such as form submissions or downloads. This data will enable you to measure the effectiveness of your content in driving desired actions.

Google Search Console

Google Search Console (or GSC) is a powerful tool for monitoring your website's performance in Google search results. Key features include:

Search Performance Reports: These reports show which keywords are driving traffic to your site, along with click-through rates and average positions in search results. Analyzing this data can help you optimize your content for better visibility.

Index Coverage: This feature provides information about which pages on your site are indexed by Google and highlights any issues that may prevent pages from appearing in search results.

Mobile Usability: GSC also assesses the mobile usability of your site, alerting you to any issues that may affect the user experience on mobile devices. Given the increasing importance of mobile optimization, addressing these issues is vital.

Social Media Analytics

If your firm shares content on social media, utilizing social media analytics tools can provide insights into how your content is performing across different platforms.

Most social media platforms, such as Facebook, X, and LinkedIn, offer built-in analytics features that allow you to track engagement metrics, including:

Post Reach: This metric indicates how many users have seen your posts. Understanding which posts have the highest reach can help you identify the types of content that resonate with your audience.

Engagement Rates: This metric tracks likes, shares, comments, and overall engagement rates to gauge how well your content is performing on social media. High engagement rates suggest that your content is resonating with your audience.

Referral Traffic: This metric monitors how much traffic your website receives from social media platforms. This data can help you assess the effectiveness of your social media strategy in driving visitors to your site.

Heatmap Tools

Heatmap tools, such as Hotjar or Crazy Egg, provide visual representations of user behavior on your website. These tools track where users click, scroll, and spend time on your pages, offering insights into how they interact with your content.

A/B Testing Tools

A/B testing tools allow you to experiment with different versions of your content to determine which performs better. This can be particularly useful for optimizing landing pages, headlines, and calls to action.

Leveraging analytics tools is essential for measuring and improving content performance. By utilizing tools like Google Analytics, Google Search Console, social media analytics, heatmap tools, and A/B testing, elder law and estate planning firms can gain valuable insights that drive meaningful results and enhance their content strategy.

Key Takeaways

- **Utilize Google Analytics:** Track audience insights, behavior flow, and content performance reports to understand how users interact with your content and identify areas for improvement.
- **Monitor Search Performance with Google Search Console:** Use search performance reports and index coverage insights to optimize your content for better visibility in search results.
- **Leverage Social Media Analytics:** Analyze engagement metrics and referral traffic from social media platforms to assess the effectiveness of your content distribution strategy.

WRAPPING UP PART 1:
MASTERING CLIENT-FOCUSED MARKETING

As we close the first part of this journey — Mastering Client-Focused Marketing — it's clear that the strategies and insights we've explored are not just about keeping up with the competition. They're about redefining what it means to be a trusted advisor in the world of elder law and estate planning.

You now have a deep understanding of your clients — grasping not just who they are but what drives them, what keeps them up at night, and how you can be the solution they're looking for. This understanding is your competitive edge, allowing you to craft messages that resonate and strategies that stick. You've learned how to communicate your firm's value in a way that cuts through the noise, using compelling content, powerful visual storytelling, and seamless user experiences to build trust and drive engagement.

But the journey doesn't stop here. In fact, you're just getting started. The insights and tools you've gained in Part 1 are designed to transform your marketing efforts, but they are also the stepping stones toward a bigger goal—building a future-focused law firm that is not only prepared to meet today's challenges but is also poised to thrive in tomorrow's landscape.

PART 2:

LEVERAGING TECHNOLOGY FOR OPERATIONAL EFFICIENCY

CHAPTER 6:

CENTRALIZED OPERATIONS FOR A SEAMLESS PRACTICE

The Benefits of Centralization

Operational efficiency isn't just a competitive advantage in this industry — it's a necessity. As such, many find that centralizing their firm's operations is a strategic move that can lead to profound improvements in both efficiency and client service.

The most compelling reason to centralize operations is the elimination of operational silos. Too often, different departments within a law firm operate independently, leading to communication breakdowns and inconsistent client experiences.

Centralization resolves many of these concerns by creating a single point of access for clients. Picture a system where all client data, documents, and communications are housed in one place. This system allows clients to track their cases, access documents, and communicate with their attorneys seamlessly, without the confusion of navigating through various departments. This unified approach also builds trust by presenting your firm as organized, responsive, and reliable.

Centralization also allows for better resource allocation. A unified system provides a clear overview of your firm's operations, helping you identify bottlenecks and optimize staff workloads. Proactive resource management not only boosts employee morale but also ensures that all clients receive the attention and timely service they deserve.

Lastly, centralization aids in compliance and risk management, which are critical in the legal industry, particularly in elder law and estate planning, where regulations around client privacy and data protection are stringent. A centralized system allows you to implement standardized procedures and protocols that ensure compliance with all relevant legal and ethical standards — reducing the risk of non-compliance and providing peace of mind to your clients.

By breaking down silos, improving data management, and fostering a collaborative environment, your firm can create a seamless, responsive practice that not only meets but exceeds client expectations. As the legal landscape continues to evolve, centralization will be key to building a future-focused law firm that is well-equipped to handle the challenges and opportunities of tomorrow.

Key Takeaways

- **Streamlined Client Experience:** Centralization breaks down operational silos, providing clients with a single point of access, leading to higher satisfaction and trust.
- **Optimized Resource Allocation**: A centralized system allows for better identification of bottlenecks and more effective redistribution of workloads, ensuring timely and efficient client service.
- **Enhanced Compliance:** Centralized operations facilitate better data analysis and ensure adherence to legal and ethical standards, which is crucial in elder law and estate planning.

Choosing the Right Tools

After you determine that centralization is right for you, it's time to select the right tools to execute.

The right technology can streamline your processes, reduce operational burdens, and enhance the quality of service you provide, positioning your firm to thrive in an increasingly competitive market.

For many, the journey to choosing the right tools begins with a comprehensive assessment of your current operations. As you do this, consider the pain points and inefficiencies that slow down your workflow. This initial assessment will guide you toward the technology that will make the most significant impact.

Key Categories of Software for Centralization

Case Management Software: At the heart of any streamlined operation is a powerful case management system. This software acts as the central hub for tracking client cases, managing deadlines, and storing essential documents. Tools like Clio and MyCase are tailored specifically for law firms, offering features like task automation, calendar integration, and comprehensive reporting.

Document Management Systems (DMS): A DMS like NetDocuments or iManage provides a secure, organized way to handle documents, offering features such as version control and electronic signatures. This type of system not only improves document retrieval times; it also ensures compliance with legal standards — protecting both your firm and your clients.

Client Relationship Management (CRM) Software: Building and maintaining strong relationships with clients is at the core of your practice. A CRM system helps track every interaction, schedule follow-ups, and store detailed client information, ensuring personalized and consistent communication. Legal-specific CRMs like Salesforce or Lawmatics are designed to enhance client relationships, making it easier to manage client data and foster long-term loyalty.

Communication Tools: Effective communication, both internally and with clients, is essential for a seamless operation. Platforms like Slack or Microsoft Teams facilitate real-time collaboration among team members, while client portals provide a secure way for clients to communicate with their attorneys and access critical information anytime.

Accounting and Billing Software: Financial management is another area where the right tools can make a significant difference. Integrating accounting software like QuickBooks with your case management system can streamline billing, invoicing, and financial tracking, reducing errors and saving time.

Marketing Automation Tools: As you centralize your operations, it's also important to streamline your marketing efforts. Tools like HubSpot or Mailchimp can automate client outreach, manage email campaigns, and track engagement metrics, helping you maintain a consistent and effective marketing presence.

Evaluating and Implementing the Right Tools

After identifying the types of tools you need, it's critical to evaluate specific software options. Focus on the following criteria to ensure that the tools you choose will meet your firm's needs:

User-Friendliness: The software you choose should be intuitive and easy to use. A complicated interface can lead to resistance from your team and reduce productivity.

Integration Capabilities: Your chosen tools should work seamlessly together. Integration between your case management system, DMS, and CRM, for example, prevents data silos and ensures that information flows smoothly between systems.

Scalability: As your firm grows, your technology needs will evolve. Ensure that the tools you select can scale with your practice, accommodating more clients and cases without sacrificing performance.

Security Features: Given the sensitive nature of client information, robust security features are non-negotiable. Prioritize tools that offer encryption, secure access controls, and compliance with data protection regulations to safeguard your clients' information.

Cost-Effectiveness: While it's important to invest in quality tools, you also need to consider your budget. Look for options that provide the best balance between features, support, and cost.

Choosing the right tools to centralize your firm requires a thorough needs assessment. Once complete, you'll have the data necessary to choose the right tools that streamline your processes and empower your team to deliver exceptional service.

Key Takeaways:

- **Assess Your Needs:** Conduct a thorough evaluation of your firm's current operations to identify pain points and areas for improvement before selecting tools.
- **Explore Software Categories:** Consider various types of software, including case management, document management, CRM, communication, accounting, and marketing automation tools to enhance your operations.
- **Evaluate Options Carefully:** When choosing software, prioritize user-friendliness, integration capabilities, scalability, security features, and cost-effectiveness to ensure a successful implementation.

Integration Strategies

The right integration strategy not only streamlines workflows — it also improves data accuracy, accessibility, and, ultimately, the quality of client service as you centralize. However, integrating multiple software solutions can be complex. Here's how to develop and implement an integration strategy that aligns with your firm's goals and enhances your practice's operational efficiency.

Define Clear Objectives

The foundation of any successful integration strategy is a clear understanding of what you hope to achieve. Start by defining specific objectives that are tailored to your firm's needs. *Are you aiming to reduce the time spent on administrative tasks, improve communication across departments, or ensure that client data is more accessible and secure?*

These goals will guide your integration efforts, helping you prioritize the systems and processes that will have the greatest impact.

Map Out Existing Processes

Before diving into integration, it's crucial to have a comprehensive understanding of your current workflows. Take the time to map out how information flows through your firm — from client intake to case resolution — and identify where bottlenecks or inefficiencies occur.

This mapping exercise will reveal critical areas where integration can streamline processes and reduce redundancy.

Choose Compatible Tools

Tool compatibility is essential for a smooth and successful integration. When selecting software solutions, prioritize those that offer built-in integrations or open APIs (Application Programming Interfaces), which facilitate seamless communication between different systems.

Prioritize Data Migration

Data migration is one of the most challenging aspects of integration, but it's also one of the most important. Moving data from legacy systems to a new, centralized platform must be done carefully to avoid data loss, corruption, or inconsistencies.

I recommend that you start this process by thoroughly cleaning your data — which involves removing duplicates, correcting errors, and standardizing formats — before migration.

A phased approach to data migration can also mitigate risks.

Consider beginning with a pilot migration using a small, representative dataset to identify potential issues. Once you've refined the process and resolved any challenges, you can proceed with full-scale migration.

Foster Collaboration Among Teams

Integration is not just a technical task; it's a collaborative effort that requires input and cooperation from various departments within your firm. It's best to involve key stakeholders from the outset to ensure that the integrated system meets the needs of all users.

Implement Training and Support

After the integration is complete, the success of your centralized system depends on how well your team can use it. Implement a comprehensive training program to ensure that all staff members understand how to operate the new system effectively.

After you train your team, consider establishing a support system where employees can access help and troubleshooting advice as they adapt to the new processes. A well-supported team will be more confident in using the integrated tools, leading to increased productivity and satisfaction.

Monitor and Optimize

Integration is not a one-and-done process; it requires continuous monitoring and optimization. I recommend that you regularly assess the performance of your integrated systems to ensure they are functioning as intended. As you do this, you can gather feedback from team members and clients to identify any persistent issues or inefficiencies that need to be addressed.

This approach ensures that your integration remains effective over time, continuously enhancing operational efficiency and client service.

Effective integration strategies are essential for building a centralized operation that enhances the efficiency and effectiveness of your elder law or estate planning practice. By defining clear objectives, mapping out existing processes, choosing compatible tools, fostering collaboration, and continuously monitoring and optimizing, your firm can successfully navigate the complexities of integration.

Key Takeaways

- **Establish Clear Objectives:** Define specific goals for integration to tailor your strategy to your firm's unique needs.

- **Map Existing Processes:** Understand current workflows to identify bottlenecks and areas for improvement before integration.
- **Choose Compatible Tools:** Ensure that the software solutions you select can integrate seamlessly to facilitate a smooth transition and enhance efficiency.

Managing Transition

Transitioning to a centralized operational model in an elder law or estate planning practice is a significant undertaking that requires meticulous planning and careful execution. The success of this transition is largely dependent on how effectively you manage the change process, ensuring that your team remains informed, engaged, and supported throughout.

Here are a few tried and tested strategies to help you navigate this critical phase, and lead your practice to a more efficient and cohesive operational structure.

Develop a Comprehensive Transition Plan

A well-structured transition plan is the cornerstone of any successful change initiative. This plan should clearly outline the steps involved in the transition, including specific timelines, assigned responsibilities, and key milestones that need to be achieved.

Breaking the transition into manageable phases—such as assessment, implementation, training, and evaluation—will help keep the process organized and manageable.

Communicate Transparently

Transparent communication is crucial during any transition. Your team needs to understand the reasons behind the move to a centralized system, the benefits it will bring, and how it will affect their day-to-day roles.

By maintaining an open dialogue, you can alleviate concerns, build trust, and foster a sense of ownership among your team members.

Regular updates through meetings, emails, or internal bulletins can keep everyone informed about the progress, address any questions or uncertainties, and provide a platform for feedback.

Celebrate Milestones

Recognizing and celebrating milestones during the transition can significantly boost team morale and reinforce a sense of accomplishment.

So, whether it's completing the initial implementation phase, achieving a specific efficiency target, or successfully training the entire team, take the time to acknowledge these achievements.

Managing the transition to a centralized operational model requires careful planning, effective communication, and continuous support. By developing a comprehensive transition plan, communicating, and celebrating milestones, you can ensure a successful transition that enhances the efficiency and effectiveness of your elder law or estate planning practice.

Key Takeaways:

- **Create a Transition Plan:** Develop a structured plan that outlines the steps, timelines, and responsibilities involved in the transition to a centralized system.
- **Communicate Openly:** Maintain transparent communication with your team to build trust and encourage collaboration throughout the transition process.
- **Provide Ongoing Support:** Establish a support system to assist team members as they adapt to the new system, ensuring a smooth transition and sustained productivity.

CHAPTER 7:
ENHANCING CLIENT COMMUNICATION

The Importance of Clear Communication
Clear communication is critical in elder law and estate planning. It lays the foundation of trust, client satisfaction, and lasting relationships.

Beyond these benefits, however, trust also demystifies the legal process for clients. Many clients entering the realm of estate planning or elder law may feel overwhelmed by the intricate legal terminology and procedures involved. By translating complex concepts into straightforward, understandable language, attorneys can empower their clients to make well-informed decisions.

Tools for Communication
The tools you use for communication can significantly impact the quality of client interactions in your elder law or estate planning practice. Selecting the right tools not only enhances efficiency but also fosters stronger relationships with clients.

Here are a few tools many firms have found success with as they work to strengthen client communications:

Client Portals

Client portals have become increasingly popular in the legal industry, providing a secure platform for clients to access their documents, case updates, and important information. These portals enhance transparency and empower clients to take an active role in their legal matters. Implementing a client portal not only improves communication but also reduces the volume of phone calls and emails, as clients can find answers to their questions independently. This self-service approach can lead to higher client satisfaction, as clients appreciate the convenience and accessibility of their information.

Video Conferencing Tools

The rise of remote work and digital communication has made video conferencing tools indispensable for legal practices. Platforms like Zoom, Microsoft Teams, or Google Meet allow attorneys to conduct virtual meetings with clients, providing a personal touch even when in-person meetings are not feasible.

Video conferencing can be particularly beneficial for initial consultations, as face-to-face interaction can help build rapport and trust. Additionally, these tools often come with features such as screen sharing and recording, which can enhance the client experience by allowing attorneys to present documents or revisit discussions later.

Instant Messaging and Collaboration Tools

Instant messaging and collaboration tools, such as Slack or Microsoft Teams, can facilitate real-time communication among team members and with clients. These platforms allow for quick exchanges of information, reducing the need for lengthy email threads and enabling faster decision-making.

Document Sharing Platforms

Secure document-sharing platforms, such as Dropbox, Google Drive, or OneDrive, are essential for facilitating collaboration and communication with clients. These tools allow attorneys to share important documents securely, ensuring that clients have access to the information they need while maintaining confidentiality.

Using document-sharing platforms also enables version control so clients can review the most up-to-date documents without confusion. They also include features for commenting and feedback, allowing for seamless collaboration on drafts and revisions.

Feedback and Survey Tools

Gathering client feedback is crucial for improving communication and service delivery. Tools like SurveyMonkey or Google Forms can be used to create client satisfaction surveys, allowing firms to gather insights into their communication practices and overall client experience.

By regularly soliciting feedback, firms can identify areas for improvement and make necessary adjustments to their communication strategies. This proactive approach not only demonstrates a commitment to client satisfaction but also fosters a culture of continuous improvement within the firm.

Leveraging the right communication tools is essential for enhancing client engagement in your elder law or estate planning practice. By implementing client portals, email management systems, video conferencing tools, instant messaging platforms, document-sharing solutions, and feedback tools, you can create a robust communication strategy that fosters transparency, responsiveness, and client satisfaction.

Key Takeaways

- **Implement Client Portals:** Use secure client portals to provide clients with easy access to their documents and case updates, enhancing transparency and engagement.
- **Utilize Video Conferencing:** Leverage video conferencing tools for virtual meetings, allowing for personal interactions and efficient communication with clients.
- **Gather Client Feedback:** Regularly solicit client feedback through surveys to identify areas for improvement and enhance your communication strategies.

Automation in Communication

Automation can be a game-changer for enhancing client communication. By automating routine tasks and communications, law firms can save time, reduce errors, and improve overall client satisfaction. However, it is essential to strike the right balance between automation and personal interaction to ensure that clients feel valued and understood.

Here are a few ways to leverage automation effectively in your communication strategies.

Automated Email Responses

One of the simplest yet most effective forms of automation is setting up automated email responses. This can be particularly useful for acknowledging client inquiries or confirming appointments.

These email sequences can be especially helpful when onboarding new clients. After a client signs an engagement letter, a series of automated emails can guide them through the next steps, provide essential information about the firm, and outline what they can expect during the process.

This proactive communication helps set clear expectations and fosters a sense of trust from the outset.

Appointment Scheduling Tools

Automating appointment scheduling can significantly enhance client convenience and reduce administrative burdens. Tools like Calendly or Acuity Scheduling allow clients to book appointments directly through an online calendar, eliminating the back-and-forth communication often associated with scheduling.

These tools can be integrated with your firm's calendar, ensuring that clients can only select available time slots.

Moreover, automated reminders can be sent to clients before their appointments, reducing the likelihood of no-shows and ensuring that clients are prepared for their meetings. This not only improves efficiency but also enhances the client experience by making scheduling straightforward and hassle-free.

Client Follow-Up Automation

Following up with clients after meetings or significant milestones is crucial for maintaining strong relationships. Automation can streamline this process by sending personalized follow-up emails or messages.

For example, after a consultation, an automated email can thank the client for their time, summarize key discussion points, and outline the next steps. They can also be scheduled for specific timeframes, such as checking in on clients after a document has been sent for review or following up on a pending matter.

This consistent communication keeps clients engaged and informed, enhancing their overall experience.

Document Generation and Delivery

Automation plays a significant role in the generation and delivery of legal documents. For example: Many practice management software solutions offer templates that can be customized based on client information. By automating document generation, attorneys can save time and reduce the risk of errors associated with manual data entry.

Once documents are generated, automated delivery systems can then ensure that clients receive their documents promptly. This workflow not only expedites the process but also enhances client satisfaction by providing timely access to important information.

Automation in communication can significantly enhance the efficiency and effectiveness of client interactions in your elder law or estate planning practice. By implementing the automation steps in this chapter, you can streamline communication processes while maintaining a personal touch.

Key Takeaways:

- **Implement Automated Responses:** Use automated email responses to acknowledge client inquiries and provide timely information, enhancing client satisfaction.
- **Streamline Appointment Scheduling:** Utilize scheduling tools to automate appointment bookings, reducing administrative burdens and improving client convenience.

- **Automate Follow-Ups and Feedback:** Implement automated follow-up communications and feedback surveys to maintain client engagement and gather valuable insights for continuous improvement.

CHAPTER 8:

DATA SECURITY AND COMPLIANCE

Understanding Data Security Basics
Data security has become a paramount concern for law firms, as sensitive client information is handled regularly. Understanding the basics of data security is essential for protecting client information, maintaining trust, and ensuring compliance with legal and ethical standards.

This chapter goes into the fundamental concepts of data security, the specific risks faced by law firms, and the measures that can be taken to safeguard sensitive information.

Common Data Security Risks
Law firms face a variety of data security risks daily, including:

Cyberattacks: Cybercriminals using this method exploit vulnerabilities in systems. Common types of attacks include phishing, ransomware, and malware. These attacks can lead to data breaches, loss of sensitive information, and significant financial losses.

Insider Threats: Not all data breaches come from external sources. Insider threats, whether intentional or accidental, can pose significant risks. For example: Employees may inadvertently expose sensitive information through careless actions, such as using unsecured devices or failing to follow security protocols.

Data Loss: Data can be lost due to hardware failures, software malfunctions, or natural disasters. Without proper backup and recovery measures, firms risk losing critical client information that may be difficult or impossible to recover.

Key Data Security Measures

To mitigate the risks above, law firms must implement robust data security measures. Here are several key strategies to consider:

Access Controls: Strict access controls to ensure that only authorized personnel can access sensitive client information. Examples of this may include using role-based access controls, requiring strong passwords, and implementing two-factor authentication.

Data Encryption: Encryption transforms data into a secure format that can only be accessed by individuals with the appropriate decryption keys.

Regular Security Audits: Regular security audits identify vulnerabilities and assess the effectiveness of your data security measures. A proactive approach in this area allows firms to address potential weaknesses before they can be exploited.

Employee Training: Educating employees about data security best practices and the importance of safeguarding client information is key to maintaining sustainable cyber health. Regular training sessions can help staff recognize potential threats, such as phishing attempts, and understand the protocols for reporting security incidents.

Data Backup and Recovery: A comprehensive data backup and recovery plan proactively protects against data loss. It's best to regularly back up critical data and ensure that backups are stored securely, both on-site and off-site. You should also test the recovery process periodically to ensure that data can be restored quickly in the event of a breach or loss.

Understanding the basics of data security is essential for law firms operating in the elder law and estate planning sectors. By recognizing the importance of data security, identifying common risks, and implementing key security measures, firms can protect sensitive client information and maintain trust.

Key Takeaways

- **Prioritize Data Security:** Recognize the importance of safeguarding client information and the potential consequences of data breaches.
- **Implement Robust Security Measures:** Use access controls, data encryption, regular audits, employee training, and backup plans to mitigate data security risks.
- **Stay Informed:** Continuously monitor the evolving landscape of data security threats and best practices to ensure your firm remains compliant and secure.

Crisis Management

No system is entirely foolproof. Despite the best efforts to implement robust security measures, breaches can still occur. Therefore, having a well-defined crisis management plan is essential for elder law and estate planning firms. This plan not only prepares your firm to respond effectively to data breaches but also helps mitigate the impact on clients and the firm's reputation.

This chapter outlines the key components of an effective crisis management strategy and the steps your firm should take to navigate a data security incident.

Preparing for a Crisis

Preparation is the cornerstone of effective crisis management. By anticipating potential data security incidents and developing a comprehensive plan, your firm can respond efficiently.

Consider these steps as you prepare your crisis management plan:

Establish an Incident Response Team: Form an incident response team composed of key personnel, including IT, legal, and communications staff. This team will be responsible for managing the response to a data breach, coordinating efforts, and ensuring that the crisis is handled effectively.

Conduct Regular Training and Drills: Regularly train your staff on the crisis management plan and conduct drills to simulate potential data breaches. These exercises help staff become familiar with the procedures and identify any gaps in the plan that need to be addressed.

Responding to a Data Breach

When a data breach occurs, a prompt and coordinated response is crucial.

Here are the key steps to take in the event of a breach:

Contain the Breach: The first priority is to contain the breach to prevent further unauthorized access to sensitive data. This may involve isolating affected systems, changing passwords, and disabling compromised accounts.

Assess the Impact: Once the breach is contained, assess the extent of the damage. Determine what data was compromised, how the breach occurred, and which clients may have been affected. This assessment will inform your next steps and communication strategy.

Notify Affected Parties: Depending on the nature of the breach and applicable regulations, you may be required to notify affected clients and regulatory authorities. Be transparent about what occurred, the data involved, and the steps your firm is taking to address the situation. Clear and timely communication is essential for maintaining trust during a crisis.

Communicating During a Crisis

Effective communication is critical during a data breach.

Here are strategies for communicating with clients and stakeholders:

Be Transparent: Honesty is key when communicating about a data breach. Provide clients with accurate information about what happened, the potential impact on their data, and the steps being taken to resolve the issue. Avoid downplaying the situation, as this can lead to further distrust.

Provide Regular Updates: Keep clients informed throughout the crisis. Regular updates on the status of the investigation, recovery efforts, and any changes to security measures can help reassure clients that your firm is taking the situation seriously.

Offer Support and Resources: Provide clients with resources to help them understand the implications of the breach and steps they can take to protect themselves. This may include offering credit monitoring services, guidance on how to change passwords, or information on recognizing phishing attempts.

Recovery and Post-Crisis Evaluation

After addressing the immediate crisis, it's essential to focus on recovery and learning from the incident.

Your firm can do this by:

Conducting a Post-Incident Review: After the crisis has passed, conduct a thorough review of the incident. Analyze what went wrong, how the breach occurred, and the effectiveness of your response. Then, you can identify areas for improvement and update your crisis management plan accordingly.

Reinforcing Security Measures: Use the insights gained from the incident to strengthen your data security measures. This may involve implementing additional security protocols, enhancing employee training, or investing in new technologies to prevent future breaches.

Communicating Lessons Learned: Share the lessons learned from the incident with your team and clients. This transparency reinforces your commitment to data security and demonstrates that your firm is taking proactive steps to prevent similar incidents in the future.

By preparing for potential crises, responding promptly, communicating transparently, and learning from incidents, your firm can mitigate the impact of data breaches and maintain client trust.

Key Takeaways:

- **Prepare a Crisis Management Plan:** Develop a comprehensive plan that outlines procedures for responding to data breaches and assign roles to an incident response team.
- **Communicate Transparently:** Be honest and transparent with clients during a crisis, providing regular updates and resources to help them protect their information.
- **Learn and Adapt:** Conduct a post-incident review to identify areas for improvement and reinforce security measures to prevent future breaches.

WRAPPING UP PART 2:
LEVERAGING TECHNOLOGY FOR OPERATIONAL EFFICIENCY

As we wrap up Part 2: Leveraging Technology for Operational Efficiency, it's clear that the integration of technology into your firm's daily operations is not just a luxury—it's a necessity.

These strategies, covered in this chapter, not only streamline your practice but also protect your client's most sensitive information, ensuring that your firm is not only efficient but also trustworthy and resilient in the face of an ever-evolving digital landscape.

However, operational efficiency and technological prowess are only part of the equation. To truly elevate your firm and deliver exceptional client service, you must cultivate a strong, values-driven culture that permeates every aspect of your practice. This is where Part 3, Building a Strong Firm Culture, comes into play.

In Part 3, we will discuss the essence of what makes a law firm not only successful but also a place where clients feel valued and supported, and where employees are motivated and aligned with the firm's mission.

As we move into this next section, get ready to explore how a strong, cohesive firm culture can be your most powerful tool for client satisfaction, team alignment, and sustainable growth.

PART 3:

BUILDING A STRONG FIRM CULTURE

CHAPTER 9:

THE ROLE OF FIRM CULTURE IN CLIENT SATISFACTION

Defining Your Firm's Culture - How to Establish a Culture that Reflects Your Firm's Values

The culture of your firm is more than just an internal ethos — it is the heartbeat of your practice that influences every client interaction and shapes your firm's reputation. A well-defined firm culture not only drives client satisfaction but also becomes the cornerstone of your firm's identity, fostering trust, loyalty, and long-term success.

To create a culture that truly reflects your firm's values, you must start by clearly articulating those values and ensuring they resonate throughout every aspect of your practice.

The process of defining your firm's culture begins with introspection and collaboration. I personally recommend that you engage your team in a meaningful dialogue about the core values that will guide your practice. This could take the form of workshops, brainstorming sessions, or surveys where team members have the opportunity to voice their thoughts on what the firm stands for and what it aspires to be. The goal of this step is to uncover and solidify core values that not only align with your mission but also inspire your team to embody these principles in their daily work.

Once your core values are clearly defined, the next step is to integrate them into your hiring processes, performance evaluations, client interactions, and even in the way you handle internal challenges.

Defining and establishing your firm's culture is not a one-time task but an ongoing process that requires dedication, reflection, and active participation from everyone within the firm. By articulating your core values, embedding them into your daily operations, and continuously celebrating them, you not only enhance client satisfaction — you also build a firm that stands strong on a foundation of shared values.

Key Takeaways

- **Articulate Core Values:** Engage your team in defining the firm's core values that align with your mission and vision.

- **Integrate Values into Operations:** Ensure that your values are reflected in hiring practices, performance evaluations, and every client interaction.
- **Celebrate and Reinforce Culture:** Make your firm's culture visible and celebrated through regular discussions, visual displays, and recognition of team members who exemplify these values.

Client-First Strategies - Techniques for Ensuring Your Culture Prioritizes Client Satisfaction

Embedding a client-first mindset into the very fabric of your firm's culture instantly sets you apart from the competition. This section explores actionable strategies to ensure your firm consistently puts clients at the forefront.

Active Listening: The Foundation of Trust

The first step in cultivating a client-first culture is to master the art of active listening. *Why?* Simply put, clients need to feel heard and understood. Active listening goes beyond merely hearing the words; however. It involves fully engaging with the client's concerns, motivations, and emotions.

Encourage your team to employ active listening techniques during every client interaction. This includes making eye contact, nodding in acknowledgment, and refraining from interrupting while the client speaks. After the client has finished, summarize what they've said to confirm understanding, ask clarifying questions to dive deeper into their concerns, and express empathy to show that you genuinely care about their situation.

These practices, when done consistently, build rapport and ensure that the client feels valued and respected — which ultimately lays the foundation for a strong, trusting relationship.

Accessibility and Responsiveness: Meeting Clients Where They Are

In the legal profession, particularly in elder law, clients often face time-sensitive issues that require prompt attention. Whether they are dealing with urgent healthcare decisions, financial planning, or end-of-life matters, clients need to know that their legal team is accessible and responsive. As such, , implementing systems that ensure timely communication is critical to maintaining a client-first culture.

My tips? Establish clear protocols for responding to client inquiries, whether they come via phone, email, or text. Then, set a firm-wide standard for response times — such as responding to all client communications within 24 hours — and make sure your team is trained to meet these expectations consistently. Lastly, consider using technology to facilitate quicker responses, such as automated email acknowledgments that let clients know their message has been received and will be addressed promptly.

Beyond just responding quickly, being accessible also means making yourself available in ways that are convenient for the client. This might involve offering flexible appointment times, including virtual consultations, which can be particularly beneficial for elderly clients or those with mobility issues.

By meeting clients where they are — both physically and emotionally — you reinforce the message that their needs are your priority.

Personalizing the Client Experience: Creating Lasting Impressions

Each client is unique, with their own set of circumstances, concerns, and aspirations. Recognizing this individuality and tailoring your approach accordingly can make a significant impact on client satisfaction.

Encourage your team to take detailed notes during client meetings and interactions, capturing both the legal aspects of the case and personal details that can be referenced in future communications. For instance, if a client mentions a family member's upcoming wedding or a recent health scare, referencing these events in follow-up conversations can demonstrate a level of care and attention that clients deeply appreciate.

Embedding a client-first culture within your firm is a strategic decision that requires intentional effort and commitment. By prioritizing active listening, ensuring accessibility and responsiveness, and personalizing the client experience, you create a practice where clients feel valued and understood. This not only leads to higher satisfaction levels but also strengthens your firm's reputation and long-term success in the competitive field of elder law and estate planning.

Key Takeaways:

- **Practice Active Listening:** Train your team to listen actively to clients, demonstrating empathy and understanding.
- **Ensure Accessibility and Responsiveness:** Implement systems for prompt communication and set response time standards to enhance client satisfaction.
- **Personalize the Client Experience:** Tailor your approach to each client's unique circumstances and remember personal details to foster loyalty.

- **Solicit and Act on Feedback:** Regularly gather client feedback to identify areas for improvement and demonstrate your commitment to their satisfaction.

Aligning Team and Mission - How to Get Your Team on Board with the Firm's Mission and Culture

A firm's mission and culture are the bedrock upon which every successful client interaction is built. However, these foundational elements are only as effective as the team that embodies them.

For your elder law or estate planning practice to truly thrive, it's essential that every team member is not only aware of but also deeply committed to the firm's mission and culture.

Aligning your team with these principles enhances morale, drives cohesion, and ultimately leads to superior client experiences and outcomes.

Communicating the Mission Clearly and Consistently

The first step in aligning your team with your firm's mission and culture is clear and consistent communication that extends far beyond a simple statement posted on the office wall or included in an employee handbook.

If you're not sure where to start, you can begin by regularly discussing the firm's mission and values during team meetings. These discussions should not be one-sided; instead, they encourage open dialogue where team members can express their interpretations of the mission and how they see it reflected in their daily work.

In addition to meetings, consider implementing tools like internal newsletters, mission-oriented workshops, or team retreats focused on culture. These platforms provide opportunities to reinforce the firm's values and mission while keeping them top-of-mind for every team member. Share success stories that highlight how the mission is being lived out, both within the firm and in client interactions.

Involving the Team in Decision-Making

A team that feels heard is a team that feels valued. Involving your team in the decision-making process is a critical strategy for fostering alignment with your firm's mission and culture.

You can do this by creating structured opportunities for team members to contribute to discussions about the firm's strategies, client service improvements, and cultural initiatives. This can be done through brainstorming sessions, advisory committees, or even informal roundtable discussions.

When decisions are made based on team input, communicate this back to the team. Let them know how their contributions influenced the final decision and what the expected outcomes are. This transparency builds trust and reinforces the idea that the team's insights are valued and integral to the firm's success.

Investing in Training and Development

Training and professional development are not just about enhancing legal skills — they are also vital for reinforcing the firm's mission and values. By investing in training programs that align with your firm's cultural goals, you equip your team with the tools they need to embody your firm's ethos in every client interaction.

While you can bring in outside vendors and support for this part, you might also consider offering workshops and training sessions that go beyond technical legal knowledge. For example, workshops on effective client communication, empathy in legal practice, and the ethical considerations unique to elder law can help team members internalize the firm's values.

All programs provided should reinforce the importance of the firm's mission while also providing practical skills that team members can apply in their day-to-day roles.

Aligning your team with your firm's mission and culture is an ongoing process that requires intentionality, communication, and investment. By clearly communicating the mission, involving your team in decision-making, and providing targeted training and development opportunities, you can foster a sense of ownership and commitment among your team members. This alignment not only enhances the internal cohesion of your firm but also translates into better client experiences and stronger, more loyal client relationships.

Key Takeaways

- **Communicate the Mission Clearly:** Regularly discuss your firm's mission and values to ensure that all team members understand and embrace them.
- **Involve the Team in Decision-Making:** Create opportunities for team members to contribute to discussions about firm strategies and initiatives, fostering a sense of ownership.
- **Invest in Training and Development:** Provide training programs that reinforce your firm's values and equip your team with the skills needed to embody the culture.

Celebrating Success - Ways to Reinforce Your Culture Through Recognition and Rewards

The culture of your firm is the glue that holds your team together and drives them toward a common mission. One of the most effective ways to solidify and reinforce this culture is by celebrating success.

Recognizing and rewarding your team members not only boosts morale but also serves as a powerful tool to reinforce the behaviors and values that align with your firm's mission.

Here are a few things to keep in mind as you work to build a culture of celebration at work.

Establish Clear Criteria for Recognition

The first step in creating a successful recognition and rewards program is establishing clear criteria for what constitutes success within your firm.

To set these criteria, consider what behaviors and outcomes are most critical to your firm's success. This could include exceptional client service, successful case outcomes, innovative contributions to firm processes, or significant teamwork efforts.

No matter what you choose, the goal is to ensure that the recognition is meaningful and directly tied to the values you wish to promote within your firm. When team members know exactly what is expected and how their efforts align with the firm's broader mission, they are more likely to strive toward those standards.

Creating a Structured Recognition Program

Once you have established clear criteria, the next step is to create a structured recognition program that regularly celebrates both individual and team successes. This program should be visible and consistent, ensuring that recognition becomes an integral part of your firm's culture.

Many firms find success by implementing monthly or quarterly awards that highlight outstanding achievements. These awards can be presented during team meetings, where the entire firm can celebrate the successes of their colleagues. Public recognition not only boosts the morale of the individual being recognized but also inspires others to strive for excellence.

Another effective strategy is to feature accomplishments in a dedicated section of your firm's internal newsletter or intranet. This allows you to spotlight successes in a way that is documented and accessible to the entire team. Or, you can incorporate a peer recognition element into your program — where team members can nominate each other for awards based on their contributions. This peer-driven approach fosters a sense of camaraderie and mutual respect, as team members feel valued not just by leadership but by their colleagues as well.

Incorporating Informal Celebrations

While formal recognition programs are essential, informal celebrations also play a crucial role in reinforcing your firm's culture. These informal gestures help create a supportive and appreciative environment that can significantly enhance team morale.

Simple actions like handwritten thank-you notes from leadership, spontaneous team lunches, or even casual team outings can make a big difference in how appreciated your team members feel. These informal celebrations do not have to be grand or costly; the key is that they are sincere and demonstrate genuine appreciation for the hard work and dedication of your team.

Celebrating success is not just about boosting morale—it's about reinforcing the values that define your firm's culture. By establishing clear criteria for recognition, creating structured programs, and incorporating informal celebrations, you foster an environment where team members feel valued and motivated to contribute to the firm's success.

Key Takeaways:

- **Establish Clear Criteria for Recognition:** Define what constitutes success in your firm, ensuring that it aligns with your values and mission.
- **Create a Structured Recognition Program:** Implement regular recognition initiatives that celebrate both individual and team achievements.
- **Incorporate Informal Celebrations:** Use informal gestures and celebrations to foster camaraderie and appreciation, enhancing team morale and cohesion.

CHAPTER 10:
MANAGING PEOPLE AND PROCESSES

Effective Team Management - Best Practices for Managing a Legal Team

The success of your firm hinges not just on individual talent but on how well that talent is managed and nurtured within a cohesive team environment. By adopting best practices that emphasize clear communication, defined expectations, and continuous professional development, you can cultivate a legal team that consistently delivers high-quality service to your clients.

Clear Communication: The Foundation of Team Success

A legal team thrives when its members feel empowered to express ideas, ask questions, and share concerns without hesitation. Establishing open lines of communication with both staff and clients ensures that everyone is on the same page, which is particularly important in a legal practice where the stakes are high and the details matter.

Setting Clear Expectations and Goals

For a legal team to function effectively, every member must understand their role and how their work contributes to the firm's overall mission. Setting clear expectations and goals is crucial for aligning the team's efforts with the firm's strategic objectives.

Begin by clearly defining each team member's responsibilities and the standards they are expected to meet. This clarity helps prevent overlap and ensures that everyone knows where they fit within the broader framework of the firm.

To further support this alignment, implement performance metrics that provide a tangible way to measure success. Key performance indicators (KPIs) such as client satisfaction rates, case resolution times, and internal collaboration levels can help track progress and identify areas for improvement. Regularly reviewing these metrics in team meetings can keep everyone focused on what matters most and provide opportunities to adjust strategies as needed.

Performance reviews are another critical tool for setting and reinforcing expectations. These reviews should be constructive, focusing not only on areas that need improvement but also on celebrating achievements. When team members see that their hard work is recognized and that there are clear pathways for professional growth, they are more likely to remain motivated and engaged.

By fostering a culture where team members feel supported, valued, and equipped to succeed, you create an environment where everyone can thrive. This not only improves the internal dynamics of your firm but also enhances the quality of service you provide to your clients.

Key Takeaways

- **Establish Open Communication:** Create an environment where team members feel comfortable sharing ideas and concerns through regular meetings and open-door policies.
- **Set Clear Expectations and Goals:** Define roles and responsibilities clearly and implement performance metrics to track progress and ensure accountability.
- **Track Progress in Public:** Performance reviews and other tools are excellent ways to involve your team in the evaluation process — encouraging them to enhance their performance collaboratively.

Delegation and Empowerment - Strategies for Empowering Your Team Through Effective Delegation

Strategic delegation is integral to successful team management, allowing you to distribute tasks efficiently, leverage your team's strengths, and ensure that the highest levels of service are maintained for your clients.

Delegation is about more than simply assigning tasks, however; it's about empowering your team to take ownership of their responsibilities — a focus which ultimately fosters a culture of accountability and enhances the overall productivity and morale of your firm.

Understanding Team Strengths and Weaknesses

The foundation of effective delegation begins with a deep understanding of your team member's strengths and areas for growth. Each person on your team brings a unique set of skills, experiences, and interests to the table. As a leader, it's your responsibility to assess these attributes and align tasks with the right individuals. This alignment not only ensures that tasks are completed efficiently but also enhances job satisfaction and professional development.

This process of matching tasks to skills is not static; it requires continuous observation and adjustment. Consider regularly reviewing your team members' performance and seek their feedback on the tasks they find most fulfilling or challenging. This dynamic approach allows you to refine your delegation strategy over time, leading to more effective teamwork and better client outcomes.

Providing Clear Instructions and Expectations
Once you've identified the right person for a task, the next crucial step is to provide clear and precise instructions. Clarity in delegation minimizes the risk of misunderstandings and sets the stage for successful task completion. When delegating, outline the specific objectives, deadlines, and any critical details that must be considered. This might include the desired outcome, key milestones, and the resources available to complete the task.

Empowering Through Autonomy and Ownership
Delegation is most effective when it's accompanied by empowerment. Empowering your team means giving them the autonomy to make decisions and encouraging them to take ownership of their tasks once delegation has taken place.

When team members feel trusted to make decisions, they are more likely to take the initiative, be innovative, and deliver higher-quality work.

Empowerment also involves recognizing and rewarding initiative. When a team member successfully takes ownership of a task and delivers exceptional results, acknowledge their effort. This recognition reinforces their sense of ownership and encourages them to continue contributing at a high level.

\Effective delegation and empowerment are crucial strategies for managing a legal team in any elder law or estate planning firm. By understanding your team's strengths, providing clear instructions, and fostering a culture of autonomy and ownership, you can enhance productivity and create a more motivated and engaged team.

Key Takeaways:

- **Assess Team Strengths:** Take the time to understand the skills and interests of your team members, ensuring tasks are delegated to those best equipped to handle them.
- **Provide Clear Instructions:** Outline objectives, deadlines, and any specific requirements clearly when delegating tasks to reduce misunderstandings.
- **Foster Autonomy and Ownership:** Empower team members by giving them the autonomy to make decisions and take ownership of their tasks, encouraging innovation and accountability.

Process Streamlining - How to Streamline Operations to Enhance Efficiency

Efficiency is not just a goal; it's a necessity. Thankfully, by systematically enhancing your operations, your firm can reduce inefficiencies, boost productivity, and ultimately deliver better service to your clients.

The process of streamlining involves assessing current workflows, leveraging technology, and establishing clear procedures that ensure consistency and efficiency across all aspects of your practice. Here are a few starting points to consider as you refine and optimize your client and staff workflows.

Assessing Current Processes

The first step in streamlining your firm's operations is to conduct a thorough assessment of your existing processes. This involves taking a close look at how work flows through your firm, from client intake to case closure.

Begin by mapping out these workflows in detail, noting each step involved in common tasks like client onboarding, document preparation, case management, billing, and follow-up communications.

As you map out these processes, look for bottlenecks. For example, if your client intake process requires multiple approvals or redundant data entry, it might be slowing down the entire process.

In addition to identifying bottlenecks, be on the lookout for redundancies. Redundant steps, such as requiring multiple team members to review the same document, waste time and increase the potential for errors. Eliminating these inefficiencies can free up valuable time that your team can use to focus on more critical tasks, like client interactions and case strategy.

Leveraging Technology for Streamlining

Technology plays a pivotal role in streamlining legal operations.

One of the most effective technological solutions for legal firms is legal management software (or an LMS).

Once installed, an LMS automates various aspects of your operations — such as document generation, time tracking, and billing. By automating these routine tasks, you reduce the administrative burden on your team, minimize errors, and ensure that work is completed faster.

Establishing Standard Operating Procedures (SOPs)

Technology alone isn't enough to streamline operations; you also need clearly defined procedures that guide how tasks are performed. This is where Standard Operating Procedures (SOPs) come in.

SOPs document the best practices for carrying out routine tasks within your firm, ensuring consistency and efficiency.

Creating SOPs begins with documenting the current best practices for each task, from client intake to case management and billing. These documents should be detailed, outlining each step of the process, the tools used, and any important considerations.

After creation, it's important to regularly review and update your SOPs to ensure they remain relevant. As technology evolves and your firm grows, processes may change — and your SOPs should reflect these changes. Regular updates ensure that your team always has access to the most current information, which helps maintain efficiency and consistency across the board.

Streamlining your firm's processes is essential for enhancing efficiency and delivering the high level of service that your clients expect. By conducting a thorough assessment of your current operations, leveraging technology to automate routine tasks, and establishing clear SOPs, you can create a more efficient and effective practice.

- **Assess Current Processes:** Map out workflows to identify bottlenecks and redundancies that hinder efficiency.
- **Leverage Technology:** Implement legal management software and CRM systems to automate routine tasks and enhance communication.
- **Establish Standard Operating Procedures:** Document best practices to ensure consistency and provide a reference for both new and seasoned team members.

Adapting to Industry Changes - How to Stay Ahead of Trends and Adjust Your Firm's Strategy Accordingly

The legal industry, especially within elder law and estate planning, is in a constant state of flux. Changes in regulations, advancements in technology, and shifting client expectations demand that law firms remain agile and responsive to maintain their relevance and competitive edge.

This task can seem overwhelming — but there are a few strategies to help simplify your process. We've included them below.

Commit to Ongoing Education and Research

A critical step in staying ahead of industry changes is fostering a culture of continuous learning within your firm. Encourage your team to engage in ongoing education and research to remain informed about the latest developments that could impact your practice. This commitment to learning ensures that your team is equipped with the knowledge and skills necessary to adapt effectively to new challenges and opportunities.

Regularly Assess and Adjust Firm Strategies

Staying ahead of industry changes also requires regular assessment and adjustment of your firm's strategies. As the legal landscape evolves, it's crucial to periodically review your service offerings, marketing efforts, and operational processes to ensure they align with current trends and client expectations.

Begin by conducting a thorough analysis of your firm's current practices. *Are there areas where your services could be expanded or improved to better meet client needs?* For instance, if you notice an increasing demand for digital solutions in estate planning, such as virtual consultations or electronic document signing, consider integrating these services into your practice. By embracing technology and adapting your offerings, you can attract a broader client base and enhance your firm's appeal.

Additionally, you should assess your marketing strategies to ensure they reflect the latest trends in client communication and engagement. For example, if social media has become a more significant tool for client outreach, consider enhancing your firm's online presence through targeted social media campaigns or by sharing informative content that positions your firm as a thought leader.

Collaborate with Industry Peers

Networking and collaboration with other legal professionals are invaluable for staying informed about industry changes. Engaging via professional organizations, networking events, and online forums can provide insights into best practices, innovative approaches, and emerging trends that might not be immediately apparent through independent research.

If you'd like other options besides LinkedIn, you can always Join relevant legal associations, such as the National Academy of Elder Law Attorneys (NAELA) or the American Bar Association's Real Property, Trust, and Estate Law Section. These organizations often offer resources, educational events, and networking opportunities that can help your firm stay connected with industry developments. Adapting to industry changes is not a one-time effort but an ongoing process that requires vigilance, flexibility, and a willingness to evolve. By committing to continuous education, regularly assessing and adjusting your firm's strategies, and collaborating with industry peers, your firm can stay ahead of trends and maintain a competitive advantage.

Key Takeaways:

- **Commit to Ongoing Education:** Encourage continuous learning within your team through research, conferences, and webinars to stay informed about industry developments.
- **Regularly Assess and Adjust Strategies:** Periodically review and refine your firm's services, marketing efforts, and operations to align with current trends and client expectations.
- **Collaborate with Industry Peers**: Engage with other legal professionals to gain insights into best practices and emerging trends that can enhance your firm's operations and service delivery.

Planning for the Future - Creating a Roadmap for Long-Term Growth and Success

The ability to strategically plan for the future is crucial for ensuring your firm's longevity and success.

Here are a few key action steps to help you start your firm's own future planning process:

Conducting a Comprehensive Assessment

The first step in creating a roadmap for future success is to conduct a thorough assessment of your firm's current position. This involves performing a SWOT analysis to evaluate your firm's strengths, weaknesses, opportunities, and threats.

Setting Clear, Measurable Goals

Once you have a clear understanding of your firm's current position, the next step is to set clear, measurable goals that align with your firm's mission and values. These goals should encompass both short-term and long-term objectives and should be specific enough to provide direction yet flexible enough to adapt to changing circumstances.

Each goal your firm sets should be accompanied by measurable outcomes, such as specific percentage increases in revenue or client satisfaction scores, to track progress and ensure accountability.

Developing a Detailed Action Plan

With your goals in place, the next step is to develop a detailed action plan that outlines the steps needed to achieve them. This plan should be comprehensive, including timelines, responsible team members, and the resources required for implementation.

Regularly reviewing and adjusting your action plan is crucial to its success. The legal landscape is continually evolving, and your firm must be agile enough to respond to changes in technology, regulations, and client expectations. By maintaining flexibility within your action plan, you ensure that your firm can pivot when necessary and stay on track toward achieving its goals.

Planning for the future is an essential component of achieving long-term growth and success in your firm. By conducting a comprehensive assessment, setting clear and measurable goals, and developing a detailed action plan, you create a roadmap that positions your firm for continued success.

Key Takeaways

- **Conduct a SWOT Analysis:** Assess your firm's strengths, weaknesses, opportunities, and threats to gain a clear understanding of its current position and potential future direction.
- **Set Clear, Measurable Goals:** Establish specific, achievable goals that align with your firm's mission and provide a framework for long-term growth and success.

- **Develop a Detailed Action Plan:** Create a comprehensive plan outlining the steps, timelines, and resources needed to achieve your goals, and review it regularly to ensure ongoing relevance and effectiveness.

WRAPPING UP PART 3:
BUILDING A STRONG FIRM CULTURE

As we wrap up Part 3: Building a Strong Firm Culture, it's evident that the foundation of any successful law firm goes beyond just operational efficiency or technological prowess. It lies in the strength of its culture — one that is deeply rooted in shared values, a commitment to client-first strategies, and a unified team that is aligned with the firm's mission.

The future of your practice depends on how well you can integrate cutting-edge technology and adapt to the rapid changes that are reshaping the legal field. This is where Part 4: Staying Ahead with Legal Technology, becomes critical.

Get ready to explore how embracing the latest legal technologies can propel your firm into the future. By the end of Part 4, you'll have the tools and knowledge to not only keep pace with the changes in the legal industry but to lead the charge, positioning your firm at the forefront of innovation and excellence.

PART 4:

STAYING AHEAD WITH LEGAL TECHNOLOGY

CHAPTER 11:

AI AND AUTOMATION IN ESTATE PLANNING & ELDER LAW

Introduction to AI in Law

Artificial Intelligence (AI) is no longer a futuristic concept; it has become an integral part of modern legal practice that's transformed the way law firms operate across various fields, including elder law and estate planning.

AI in itself refers to the simulation of human intelligence processes by machines, particularly computer systems; which can perform tasks such as learning, reasoning, problem-solving, understanding natural language, and recognizing patterns.

For law firms, especially those focusing on elder law, AI offers a myriad of opportunities to enhance efficiency, improve accuracy, and provide better client service.

For example: AI-driven tools can assist with extensive legal research by quickly scanning through vast amounts of case law, statutes, and legal precedents, identifying relevant information that might otherwise take hours or even days to uncover manually. This not only accelerates the research process but also enhances the thoroughness of the legal analysis, ensuring that no critical detail is overlooked.

AI can also predict case outcomes by analyzing historical data, allowing attorneys to advise clients with greater confidence and clarity.

However, integrating AI into legal practice is not without its challenges. Elder law firms must navigate the complexities of adopting new technologies while ensuring that they maintain the personal touch that is so crucial in this field.

The key to successfully incorporating AI lies in understanding its capabilities and limitations and strategically integrating these tools to complement, rather than replace, the human elements of legal practice.

Ethical Considerations

While AI's benefits in elder law are substantial, they must be balanced with careful consideration of ethical implications. The legal profession is built on principles of justice, confidentiality, and client trust, and the use of AI introduces new ethical challenges that must be navigated with caution.

One of the primary ethical concerns is the potential for AI to perpetuate existing biases. AI systems are often trained on historical data, and if that data reflects biases — such as those based on race, gender, or socioeconomic status — the AI system may inadvertently reinforce these biases in its predictions or recommendations. For elder law firms, which often deal with vulnerable populations, it is crucial to ensure that AI tools are used in a way that upholds the principles of fairness and equity.

Confidentiality and data security must also be considered when implementing AI in a legal practice. Elder law attorneys routinely handle sensitive client information, including financial records, healthcare directives, and personal identification details. When using AI tools to process this data, firms must ensure that robust security measures are in place to protect against unauthorized access or data breaches.

Transparency in the use of AI is critical. Clients should be informed when AI tools are being used in their cases, and they should understand the potential benefits and limitations of these technologies. This transparency helps build trust and ensures that clients feel comfortable with the technology being employed in their legal matters.

Choosing the Right Tools

Selecting the right AI tools for your elder law practice requires a thoughtful and strategic approach. The first step is to assess the specific needs of your firm and identify the areas where AI can have the most significant impact.

When evaluating AI tools, consider factors such as ease of use, integration with existing systems, and the level of customer support provided by the vendor. A user-friendly interface is crucial, particularly for firms that may not have extensive technical expertise. The chosen tools should also seamlessly integrate with your current practice management software to ensure a smooth transition and avoid disruptions to your workflow.

Cost is another important consideration for your firm's AI tool suite. While some AI solutions may require a significant upfront investment, the long-term benefits in terms of efficiency, accuracy, and client satisfaction can outweigh the initial costs. Thankfully, many AI vendors offer tiered pricing models, allowing firms to start with a basic package and scale up as needed.

As elder law and estate planning practices continue to evolve, the integration of AI and automation will play an increasingly vital role in maintaining competitive advantage and delivering exceptional client service.

By staying informed, choosing the right tools, and navigating the ethical challenges thoughtfully, your firm can harness the power of AI to drive growth, efficiency, and innovation.

Key Takeaways:

- **Embrace AI for Efficiency:** AI can streamline research, document generation, and client interactions, allowing elder law firms to operate more efficiently and effectively.
- **Navigate Ethical Challenges:** Be mindful of biases, confidentiality, and transparency when implementing AI tools to ensure ethical compliance and build client trust.
- **Choose Wisely:** Assess your firm's needs, consider integration and support, and involve your team in selecting AI tools that will enhance your practice.

CHAPTER 12:
THE FUTURE OF LEGAL PRACTICE

Scalable Technology Solutions

In the evolving landscape of elder law and estate planning, the ability to scale operations effectively is essential for sustaining long-term success. Scalable technology solutions are designed to grow alongside your firm, enabling you to adapt to changes in client needs, regulatory requirements, and market conditions without the need for significant overhauls.

One of the most significant advantages of scalable technology is its capacity to handle increasing workloads without compromising performance. As your firm grows — whether through an expanding client base, the addition of new practice areas, or geographic expansion — your technological infrastructure must be able to support this growth seamlessly.

This is particularly critical in elder law, where the intricacies of estate planning, Medicaid planning, and guardianship cases demand robust and reliable systems.

Cloud-based solutions are a prime example of scalable technology that offers both flexibility and accessibility. By leveraging the cloud, your firm can ensure that all critical data and tools are available whenever and wherever they are needed. This is especially important in elder law, where attorneys often need to meet clients in various locations, such as nursing homes or clients' homes.

A cloud-based practice management system can streamline case management, billing, and communication, ensuring that attorneys have the tools they need at their fingertips, no matter where they are.

Innovative Practices

The legal industry is ripe for innovation, and elder law firms that embrace new technologies and practices can set themselves apart from the competition. Innovative practices not only enhance service delivery but also contribute to client satisfaction and retention, which are particularly important in a field as personal as elder law.

One of the most transformative innovations in recent years is the development of comprehensive client portals.

These portals provide clients with 24/7 access to their legal documents, case updates, and direct communication with their attorneys. For elder law clients who may be dealing with stressful and emotional situations, having easy access to information can be incredibly reassuring.

Another cutting-edge practice involves the use of virtual reality (VR) for client consultations. Imagine an elder law firm using VR technology to simulate various estate planning scenarios, allowing clients to visualize the impact of their decisions on their loved ones and assets!

These innovative practices demonstrate that the strategic use of technology is not just about keeping pace with the industry; it's about fundamentally enhancing the way law firms operate and interact with clients. By embracing innovation, elder law firms can provide more personalized, effective, and responsive services, ultimately leading to stronger client relationships and sustained growth.

It's clear that the future of elder law and estate planning is tied to the adoption of advanced technologies. We've explored how AI and automation can revolutionize the way you manage your practice, from streamlining research and document generation to enhancing client interactions. We've also discussed the importance of scalable technology solutions, the potential of innovative practices like virtual reality and blockchain, and the emerging trends that will shape the legal landscape in the years to come. These technological advancements are not just tools — they are catalysts that can propel your firm to new heights, enabling you to deliver more efficient, accurate, and client-centered services.

However, while technology is a powerful enabler, it is only one piece of the puzzle. The success of your firm also hinges on how well you communicate your unique value to clients and the broader market as the competition increases. After all — Your brand is more than just a logo or a tagline — it's the embodiment of your firm's identity, values, and promise to your clients. It's what sets you apart from the competition and what makes clients choose your firm over others.

This is where Part 5: Building a Stand-Out Brand, comes into play.

In Part 5, we'll take a deep dive into the strategies that can help you define and communicate a compelling brand identity that resonates with your target audience.

As we transition into this final part of the book, get ready to unlock the secrets to building a brand that not only stands out in the crowded legal marketplace but also resonates deeply with your clients.

PART 5:

BUILDING A STAND-OUT BRAND

CHAPTER 13:

DEFINING AND COMMUNICATING YOUR BRAND

Today, standing out in the field of elder law and estate planning requires more than just offering excellent legal services. It requires a strong, well-defined brand that not only captures the essence of your firm but also resonates deeply with your target audience. Your brand is not just a logo, a slogan, or a color scheme; it embodies your firm's values, your approach to client service, and the unique benefits you provide to those who trust you with their most sensitive legal matters.

In this chapter, we will explore how to create a compelling brand identity that reflects your firm's core values, ensures consistency across all platforms, leverages the power of storytelling, and evolves as your firm grows.

Creating a Brand Identity

Your brand identity is the cornerstone of how your firm is perceived by the world. It's the visual, emotional, and psychological representation of your firm, encapsulating everything that makes your practice unique. A strong brand identity not only distinguishes your firm from the competition but also builds a connection with clients who share your values and trust your expertise.

Crafting Your Unique Value Proposition

At the heart of your brand identity lies your Unique Value Proposition (UVP). This is the clear, concise statement that articulates the unique benefits your firm offers and why clients should choose you over other options.

Crafting a powerful UVP requires a deep understanding of your firm's strengths and the specific needs of your target audience.

For an elder law and estate planning firm, for example, your UVP might emphasize your deep expertise in complex estate issues, your compassionate approach to client service, or your innovative use of technology to streamline legal processes. Or, perhaps, it's your extensive experience in handling sensitive elder care matters, your reputation for personalized service, or your commitment to using the latest legal technologies to enhance client outcomes.

Whatever it is, your UVP should clearly communicate how your firm meets the unique needs of your clients and why that matters to them.

Visual Branding Elements

While your UVP forms the core of your brand's messaging, your visual branding elements — such as your logo, color scheme, typography, and imagery — are what make that message visually compelling and memorable. These elements should be carefully designed to reflect your firm's values and to create a consistent brand experience across all touchpoints.

No matter what you choose here, know this: The key is consistency. Every piece of visual communication, from your website to your social media profiles to your office signage, should reflect the same brand identity, creating a cohesive and recognizable experience for your clients.

Communicating Your Brand Story

Beyond your visual elements and UVP, your brand story is what gives your firm a human face and connects with clients on an emotional level. It's the narrative that explains who you are, what drives you, and why you do what you do. It's an opportunity to share your firm's history, your successes, and the impact you've had on your clients' lives.

In the context of elder law and estate planning, your brand story might highlight your firm's commitment to helping families navigate difficult decisions with dignity and compassion. You could share stories of how you've helped clients protect their loved ones' futures or how your innovative solutions have made a difference in their lives.

By telling your story authentically, you not only build trust and credibility but also create a connection with your audience that goes beyond the transactional nature of legal services. This also differentiates your firm in a competitive market, builds credibility and trust, and attracts clients who align with your values and offerings.

Key Takeaways

- **Present Yourself Well:** Your brand identity is the essence of your firm, encompassing your values, mission, and unique value proposition.
- **Be Clear, Be Powerful:** Craft a compelling, unique value proposition that clearly communicates the benefits of choosing your firm over others.
- **Maintain Reliability:** Consistency in your visual branding elements is key when it comes to creating a cohesive and memorable brand experience across all client touchpoints.

- **Share Boldly:** Share your brand story authentically to connect with your audience on a deeper level, building trust and long-term loyalty.

Brand Voice Consistency

Your brand voice is the distinct personality and tone that comes through in all your communications, from client emails to social media posts. It reflects who you are as a firm, what you stand for, and how you wish to be perceived by clients and prospects alike.

When executed well, a consistent brand voice fosters recognition, builds trust, and strengthens the relationship between your firm and those you serve.

In this section, we'll explore the techniques necessary to maintain a consistent and impactful brand voice across all platforms, ensuring that your firm presents a unified and professional image.

Establishing Your Brand Voice

The first step in achieving brand voice consistency is to clearly define what your brand voice is. This requires a deep understanding of your firm's core values, mission, and the type of relationship you want to build with your clients.

To begin, ask yourself: *Are we a firm that clients see as a formal and authoritative guide through complex legal matters, or do we aim to be more approachable, offering compassionate support during difficult times? Do we use formal legal jargon to emphasize our expertise, or do we prefer plain, accessible language to make our services more inclusive and understandable?*

For example: If your firm's mission centers around providing clear, compassionate guidance to elderly clients and their families, your brand voice should be warm, empathetic, and reassuring. Every piece of communication should reflect this tone, whether it's a blog post explaining the nuances of estate planning, or a social media update celebrating a client success story.

By establishing a brand voice that aligns with your firm's values and mission, you create a consistent and authentic communication style that resonates with your audience and reinforces your firm's identity.

Tone and Style Guidelines

Once you've defined your brand voice, the next step is to codify it into tone and style guidelines that can be consistently applied across all forms of communication. These guidelines serve as a reference tool for everyone in your firm, ensuring that all messaging aligns with the established brand identity — regardless of who is crafting the message or where it's being shared.

These guidelines should cover key elements such as:

Language Preferences: Specify whether your firm prefers formal or informal language. *Should you use legal jargon to emphasize expertise, or is it better to simplify terms for broader accessibility?*

Tone Variations: Outline how your tone might shift depending on the context. For example: Client communications might be more compassionate and personalized, whereas professional blogs might adopt a more authoritative tone.

Grammar and Punctuation Rules: Consistency in grammar and punctuation not only reflects professionalism; it also contributes to a unified voice. Here, you'll decide on preferences for elements such as Oxford commas, sentence structure, and capitalization.

Examples of Preferred Communication:
Providing concrete examples of how to handle specific situations — like responding to client inquiries, crafting social media posts, or writing case summaries — can help team members understand how to apply the brand voice in real-life scenarios.

By creating a comprehensive style guide that addresses these elements, your firm can ensure that every piece of communication feels consistent and reinforces your brand identity.

Tailoring Your Voice to Different Platforms

While consistency is crucial, it's also important to recognize that different platforms may require slight adjustments to your brand voice. The way you communicate on LinkedIn, for example, will likely differ from how you engage on Facebook, Instagram, or in client emails.

Adapting your voice to fit the context and audience of each platform ensures that your message is both appropriate and effective, while still remaining true to your firm's overarching brand personality.

The key to managing these shifts well is to maintain the core elements of your brand voice — such as empathy, clarity, and professionalism — while adapting to the nuances of what your clients expect on each platform.

Training and Feedback

Ongoing training is key to maintaining brand voice consistency.

Consider offering workshops or training modules that cover the brand style guide, providing hands-on practice in applying the tone and style guidelines across different types of communication. You can also encourage team members to bring real examples of their work for review and discussion, highlighting both successes and areas for improvement.

This collaborative approach not only improves consistency but also fosters a stronger sense of unity and purpose within the team.

Key Takeaways:

- **Define Your Brand Voice:** Clearly articulate your firm's personality, values, and the desired relationship with your audience to establish a consistent communication style.
- **Create a Brand Style Guide:** Develop comprehensive tone and style guidelines to ensure uniformity in communication across all platforms.
- **Adapt Your Voice Appropriately:** Tailor your brand voice to fit the context and audience of different platforms while maintaining core elements of your identity.
- **Invest in Training and Feedback:** Provide ongoing training and constructive feedback to ensure that all team members embody the brand voice in their interactions.

Storytelling in Branding

Storytelling is a powerful tool that can elevate your brand beyond mere words and visuals and create an emotional connection with your audience.

In this section, we will explore how to harness the art of storytelling to craft a compelling brand narrative that engages and inspires.

The Power of Storytelling

Stories have the ability to captivate, inspire, and evoke empathy in ways that facts and figures cannot. When you tell a story, you create a memorable and relatable experience for your audience, allowing them to connect with your firm on a deeper level. This connection is particularly vital in the realm of elder law and estate planning, where clients often face emotionally charged decisions.

Identifying Your Brand Story

Your brand story is more than just a chronological account of your firm's history. It is the narrative that communicates who you are, what you stand for, and why you do what you do. To identify your brand story, consider the following questions:

What inspired you to start your firm? Sharing this inspiration can help potential clients understand your dedication to the field.

What values drive your practice? Reflect on the core values that guide your firm's approach to client service and legal practice.

How have you made a difference in your client's lives? Highlight specific examples where your firm has had a positive impact on your clients. These stories serve as powerful testimonials to your firm's ability to navigate complex legal landscapes and deliver meaningful results.

What challenges have you overcome to reach where you are today? Every firm faces challenges, whether it's adapting to new regulations, handling particularly difficult cases, or growing the practice in a competitive market. Sharing how you've overcome these obstacles can demonstrate resilience and reinforce your firm's commitment to excellence.

Elements of a Compelling Brand Narrative

A compelling brand narrative typically includes the following elements:

Character: You, as the founder or your key team members, are the guides in your brand story. Highlight your personality, expertise, and passion for helping clients navigate elder law and estate planning challenges. The hero in your story is your client. They are the main characters. By putting a human face to your firm, you make it easier for clients to connect with you on a personal level, and hire you as their guide!

Conflict: Every good story has conflicts or challenges that need to be overcome. Here, you can share the obstacles you've helped people just like them face, such as complex legal cases, changing regulations, or client crises, and how you've navigated them successfully. This section showcases authenticity, transparency, and your problem-solving abilities — all of which amount to dedication to your clients.

Resolution: The resolution of your brand story should showcase the positive outcomes and successes you've achieved for your clients. These entries could include testimonials, case studies, and client success stories to demonstrate the impact of your work.

Storytelling Across Different Channels

Storytelling can be integrated into various aspects of your branding, including your website, social media posts, client communications, and marketing materials. Here are a few different ways you can use storytelling to humanize and elevate your firm in the minds of your clients.

Client Testimonials: These are real stories from the people you've helped, providing powerful evidence of your firm's impact. You can share these testimonials across your website, social media, and promotional materials.

Team Profiles: In this form of storytelling, you can highlight the stories of your team members — calling out what brought them to elder law or estate planning, what they enjoy about their work, and how they contribute to the firm's success. This form of storytelling not only builds rapport with clients but also strengthens the overall narrative of your firm.

Behind-the-Scenes Glimpses: Offering a behind-the-scenes look at your firm's operations, whether through videos, blog posts, or social media updates, can make your practice more relatable and transparent.

By embracing storytelling in your branding efforts, you can create a compelling narrative that resonates with your audience, differentiates your firm, and fosters meaningful connections with clients and prospects. This narrative then becomes the backbone of your brand, driving engagement, loyalty, and long-term success in the competitive world of elder law and estate planning.

Key Takeaways

- **Storytelling Humanizes Your Brand:** Use storytelling to create emotional connections with your audience, making your firm more relatable and memorable.
- **Identify Your Unique Brand Story:** Uncover and share the aspects of your journey, how you help clients, and the values that set your firm apart from competitors.
- **Craft a Compelling Narrative:** Incorporate characters, conflict, and resolution into your brand story to engage and inspire your audience.
- **Integrate Storytelling Across Channels:** Use storytelling in various communication platforms to showcase your expertise, build trust, and connect with clients on an emotional level.

Rebranding and Evolution

Firms must be willing to adapt and evolve to meet the changing needs of clients and stay relevant in a competitive market. Rebranding, in this context, is not just about changing your logo or color scheme; it's a strategic process that involves reassessing your firm's identity, values, and positioning to better align with your target audience and business goals.

In this section, we will explore when and how to consider rebranding, the steps involved in the rebranding process, and how to evolve your brand as your firm grows.

Knowing When to Rebrand

Rebranding is a significant decision that should be driven by a clear purpose and strategic vision. It's not something to be taken lightly, as it requires time, resources, and a deep understanding of your firm's current position in the market. However, when done correctly, rebranding can breathe new life into your practice and open doors to new opportunities.

Consider rebranding when:

Your firm's current brand no longer reflects your values, services, or target audience:

As your firm evolves, the original brand you established may no longer fully represent who you are or what you offer. These shifts are natural and healthy — however, in the event of ongoing changes, your brand should reflect said changes.

You are expanding your services or entering new markets: As your firm grows and begins offering new services or targeting new demographics, your brand must evolve to encompass those changes as well.

Your firm has undergone significant formative changes: Major transitions such as mergers, leadership changes, or a shift in the firm's mission can signal the need for a rebrand. These changes often bring about new goals and directions, which your brand should align with to maintain cohesion and clarity.

Client demographics or preferences shift: As the needs and preferences of your clients change, your brand should adapt accordingly. For example, if you notice that your client base is becoming more tech-savvy, it may be time to update your brand messaging and services to emphasize your digital capabilities.

New technologies or industry trends emerge: The legal industry is constantly evolving, with new technologies and trends reshaping how services are delivered. If your firm adopts new technologies — such as virtual consultations or AI-driven legal research — your brand should reflect this modern approach.

Significant milestones are achieved: Major achievements, such as expanding to new locations, launching innovative services, or receiving industry recognition, can serve as catalysts for brand evolution. These milestones provide an opportunity to refresh your brand and highlight your firm's growth and success.

Remember: *Rebranding is not about change for the sake of change but about strategically positioning your firm for future success.*

The Rebranding Process

The rebranding process typically involves several critical steps, each of which plays a vital role in ensuring a successful transition:.

Assessment: Before you rebrand, start by evaluating your current brand identity, market positioning, and client perceptions. As you assess, conduct a SWOT analysis (exploring your brand's strengths, weaknesses, opportunities, and threats) to gain a clear understanding of where your brand currently stands, what's working well, and what needs improvement.

Strategy Development: Once you have a clear understanding of your brand's current position, it's time to define your rebranding goals. *What do you hope to achieve with this rebrand? Are you aiming to attract a new demographic, reposition your firm in the market, or simply modernize your brand's appearance?* Alongside these goals, you'll need to develop a clear strategy that includes target audience identification, messaging, and visual elements.

Implementation: With your strategy in place, begin rolling out your rebranding across all touchpoints. This includes updating your website, social media profiles, marketing materials, office signage, and any other place your brand appears. Consistency is key during this phase—ensure that all visual elements, messaging, and tone align with your new brand identity.

Communication: Effective communication is essential during the rebranding process, both with clients and internal stakeholders. As you go, clearly explain the reasons behind the rebranding, the benefits it brings, and how it aligns with your firm's mission and values. This transparency helps maintain trust and ensures a smooth transition.

Whether you are refreshing your brand to appeal to a new demographic or modernizing your visual identity to reflect technological advancements, rebranding offers a powerful way to position your firm for future success.

Key Takeaways:

- **Rebranding Should Be Purpose-Driven:** Rebranding should be driven by a clear purpose, strategic vision, and alignment with your firm's goals.
- **Follow a Strategic Process:** The rebranding process involves assessment,

strategy development, implementation, and communication to ensure a seamless transition.
- **Evolve Proactively:** Continuously evolve your brand to reflect changes in client demographics, industry trends, and internal developments.
- **Position for Growth:** Strategic rebranding can position your firm for growth, attract new clients, and ensure long-term success in a competitive market.

CHAPTER 14:
LEVERAGING OWNED MEDIA TO AMPLIFY YOUR MESSAGE

Building Your Digital Presence

Your firm's digital presence is more than just a necessity; it's a critical element of your marketing strategy and client engagement. In fact, a strong digital presence can be the factor that differentiates you from competitors and establishes you as a go-to resource for your clients.

This section will guide you through the key strategies needed to build a digital presence that not only attracts potential clients but also reinforces your firm's reputation as an authority in your field.

Website Optimization

Your website is the cornerstone of your digital presence — and it's where most potential clients will form their first impressions of your firm.

Here's a quick list of touchpoints to consider before launching or publishing your website, allowing you to get off to the best possible start with your customers.

User Experience (UX) and Design: Start by making your website easy to navigate implementing a clean design that reflects the professionalism of your firm. UX dictates that pages should load quickly, and the design should be responsive, meaning it adjusts seamlessly for mobile devices. Additionally, given that many potential clients may be accessing your site from a smartphone or tablet, a mobile-friendly design is crucial.

Content and Clarity: The content on your website should clearly communicate who you are, what you do, and how you can help. For example: Your homepage should succinctly convey your firm's unique value proposition, services, and contact method. You also might include a "Frequently Asked Questions" section to address common client concerns, which can improve your site's search engine rankings by incorporating relevant keywords naturally.

Client Testimonials and Case Studies: Trust is vital in elder law and estate planning, and there's no better way to build trust than by showcasing the positive experiences of your past clients. You can feature client testimonials prominently on your homepage or create a dedicated page for success stories.

Educational Resources: Consider adding a resources section where visitors can download informative guides, checklists, or white papers. These resources can help educate potential clients on important topics related to elder law and estate planning, positioning your firm as a thought leader in the field.

Blogging and Content Creation: A well-maintained blog can establish your firm as an authority in elder law and estate planning, drive organic traffic to your website, and provide a platform for engaging with your audience on topics that matter to them.

Email Marketing: This form of marketing remains one of the most effective tools for maintaining relationships with clients, nurturing leads, and staying top-of-mind with your audience. By building a robust email list and delivering valuable, relevant content directly to your subscribers' inboxes, you can foster long-term relationships and drive conversions.

Lead Magnets: Start by offering valuable content or resources in exchange for contact information. This could be a downloadable guide on estate planning basics or a checklist for preparing for a legal consultation. Ensure that your email sign-up forms are easy to find on your website, and consider offering incentives such as exclusive access to webinars or free consultations.

Segmenting Your Audience: Not all clients and prospects have the same needs, so it's important to segment your email list based on factors such as their stage in the client journey, their interests, or the services they are most likely to need. This allows you to send targeted emails that are more likely to resonate with each group, increasing the effectiveness of your campaigns.

By focusing on building and optimizing your digital presence through these strategies, your firm can increase its online visibility, attract more clients, and solidify its position as a trusted leader in elder law and estate planning.

Key Takeaways

- **Your Website is the Foundation:** Optimize your website for user experience and search engines to ensure it effectively represents your firm and attracts potential clients.
- **Content is King:** Publish valuable content through blogging and other formats to establish

thought leadership and engage with your audience.
- **Email Marketing is Essential:** Use email marketing to maintain relationships, nurture leads, and keep your audience informed and engaged.
- **SEO is Critical:** Implement strong SEO strategies to improve your online visibility and attract qualified traffic to your website.

Using Social Media Effectively

Social media is an indispensable tool for elder law and estate planning firms looking to connect with clients, share valuable content, and build lasting relationships.

In this section, we will explore best practices for leveraging social media to elevate your firm's online presence and create deeper connections with clients and prospects.

Choosing the Right Platforms

The first step in creating an effective social media strategy is choosing the platforms that align with your firm's goals and resonate with your target audience. Not every platform will be suitable for your practice, so it's crucial to focus on those that offer the most potential for reaching and engaging your specific client base.

LinkedIn: As a professional networking platform, LinkedIn is ideal for sharing industry insights, connecting with other professionals, and building relationships with referral sources. It's a great place to establish your firm's authority in elder law by posting thought leadership articles, updates on legal trends, and firm achievements.

Facebook: With its broad user base, Facebook is an excellent platform for building community, sharing educational content, and engaging directly with clients and prospects. Through Facebook, you can post updates, host live sessions, share success stories, and interact with followers who may have questions or need legal guidance.

X: X's real-time nature makes it perfect for sharing industry news, quick updates, and engaging in conversations with a wide audience. It's also a good platform for participating in relevant hashtags or legal discussions, helping to increase your visibility among peers and potential clients.

Instagram: While traditionally more visual, Instagram offers opportunities to showcase your firm's culture, behind-the-scenes glimpses, and the personal side of your practice. This platform is particularly effective for humanizing your brand through imagery and making your firm more relatable.

YouTube: As video content continues to dominate online engagement, YouTube serves as a powerful tool for sharing educational videos, client testimonials, webinars, and more. Its user-friendly interface allows you to provide in-depth explanations of complex legal topics in a way that's accessible and engaging for your audience.

Content Curation and Creation

A successful social media strategy balances curated and original content, providing your audience with a mix of valuable information and unique insights that demonstrate your firm's expertise.

Curated Content: Sharing content from reputable sources, such as news articles, industry reports, and expert opinions, helps position your firm as a well-informed participant in the elder law and estate planning fields.

Original Content: Creating your own content allows you to directly address the specific needs and concerns of your audience. This could include blog posts that break down complex legal concepts, infographics that visualize key information, or videos where you discuss common elder law issues.

By producing content that is tailored to your audience, you reinforce your firm's brand and provide valuable resources that keep your followers engaged.

Rather than adopt a fractional approach, I recommend that you consider developing a content calendar for your firm that ensures a consistent mix of both curated and original content. This approach not only helps you stay organized but also ensures that your social media channels remain active and relevant to your audience.

Engagement and Community Building

Social media is as much about engagement as it is about content. To build a strong, loyal community around your firm, you must actively engage with your audience.

Engagement typically falls into two primary camps:

Responsive Interaction: This type of interaction occurs when you respond promptly to comments, messages, and inquiries on your social media platforms.

Fostering Discussions: This type of interaction encourages discussions by asking questions, posting polls, or inviting followers to share their experiences related to elder law and estate planning. This approach not only increases engagement but also helps you gain insights into what matters most to your audience.

Analytics and Performance Tracking

Tracking your dashboard analytics helps you to maximize the effectiveness of your social media efforts.

Many do this using analytics tool suites. Most social media platforms offer built-in analytics tools that provide insights into how your content is performing. Metrics provided, such as post engagement, follower growth, click-through rates, and audience demographics, can help you understand what resonates with your audience and where there's room for improvement.

By using social media effectively, you can not only amplify your firm's message but also foster deeper connections with your audience, ultimately leading to increased brand loyalty and client engagement.

Key Takeaways:

- **Choose the Right Platforms:** Focus on social media platforms that align with your firm's goals and where your audience is most active.
- **Curate and Create Content**: Use a mix of curated and original content to provide valuable information and showcase your firm's expertise.
- **Engage and Build Community:** Actively interact with your audience to build relationships,

foster discussions, and strengthen client connections.
- **Track and Optimize:** Regularly analyze your social media performance to refine your strategy and maximize impact.

Influencer Partnerships and Collaborations

Partnering with influencers, industry experts, or complementary businesses can be an effective way to expand your content's reach and tap into new audience segments.

Additionally, influencers and thought leaders in the elder law or broader legal community often have pre-established followings that trust their recommendations, making them valuable allies in amplifying your message.

Here are a few ways you can leverage influencers in your marketing strategy:

Co-Creating Content: Collaborate with influencers or experts to co-create content, such as blog posts, videos, or webinars.

Joint Webinars and Events: Hosting joint webinars or live events with influencers or complementary businesses can draw a larger, more diverse audience. Additionally, these events provide a platform for in-depth discussions,

Q&A sessions, and networking opportunities, all of which enhance your firm's visibility and reputation.

Guest Appearances: Consider making guest appearances on popular podcasts or video channels within the legal or elder care community.

Paid Promotion and Advertising

Paid promotion and advertising significantly boosts the visibility of your content; particularly in a crowded online space. Many firms turn to paid advertising to generate relevant leads and to boost traffic over different critical time periods.

Here are a few common areas you can invest in as you begin to launch your paid initiatives:

Social Media Ads: Platforms like Facebook, LinkedIn, and Instagram offer advanced targeting options for paid advertisers, allowing you to promote your content to specific audiences based on factors such as location, age, interests, and behaviors. You can then use these ads to drive traffic to your workshops, webinars, blog posts, videos, or landing pages.

Google AdWords: Pay-per-click (PPC) advertising through Google AdWords helps you reach potential clients who are actively searching for elder law or estate planning services. You'll do this by bidding on relevant keywords that your clients are searching, ensuring your content appears at the top of search engine results pages.

Sponsored Content: Sponsored articles or posts expose your content to a wider audience and position your firm as a leading voice in the field. As such, many firms invest in sponsored content on industry websites, blogs, or newsletters.

Native Advertising: Native ads blend seamlessly into the content of a website or platform, making them less intrusive and more likely to engage readers.

Key Takeaways:

- **Multi-Channel Distribution:** Diversify content distribution across multiple channels to maximize visibility and engagement.
- **Repurpose Content:** Repackage existing content into different formats to extend its reach and reinforce key messages.
- **Collaborate for Reach:** Partner with influencers and industry experts to tap into new audience segments and amplify your message.
- **Invest in Paid Promotion:** Use targeted advertising to boost content visibility, drive traffic, and generate leads effectively.

Creating a Referral Network

Referrals serve as the lifeblood of many successful legal practices, bringing in a steady stream of new clients and validating your firm's reputation and expertise.

When clients and professional contacts refer others to your firm, they are essentially endorsing your services, which carries far more weight than traditional advertising.

So, by cultivating and nurturing relationships with key referral sources, you can create a network that continuously drives growth and positions your firm as a trusted authority in the industry.

Identifying Referral Sources

The first step in creating a successful referral network is identifying potential referral sources. These sources can be varied and may include:

Existing Clients: Satisfied clients are often your best advocates. Encourage them to refer friends, family, and colleagues who may need your services. A personal recommendation from a trusted friend or family member can be incredibly persuasive.

Professional Networks: Other professionals, particularly those in related fields, can be excellent referral sources. For example: Financial advisors, accountants, and insurance agents often work with clients who could benefit from elder law and estate planning services.

Community Organizations: Organizations that serve the elderly or those planning for their future (such as senior centers, retirement communities, and nonprofits focused on elder care) can be valuable referral partners.

Healthcare Providers: Doctors, geriatric care managers, and other healthcare professionals frequently encounter patients who need legal assistance with elder law issues. Building relationships with these providers can lead to a steady stream of client referrals.

Legal Professionals in Other Specialties: Lawyers who practice in areas such as family law, real estate law, or personal injury law might not specialize in elder law but can refer clients who need services you offer.

Providing Value to Referral Partners

To encourage referral partners to recommend your firm consistently, it's essential to provide value in the relationship. This involves:

Creating Educational Resources: Offer your referral partners access to educational materials that they can share with their clients, such as brochures, guides, or newsletters. These resources not only help their clients, but they also reinforce the value of the partnership.

Networking Opportunities: Host events, such as seminars or workshops, that bring together professionals from various fields. These events provide value to your referral partners by offering them opportunities to expand their own networks and knowledge.

Reciprocal Referrals: Whenever possible, refer clients to your partners who could benefit from their services. This mutual exchange of referrals strengthens the relationship and shows that you're committed to a reciprocal partnership.

Regular Updates: Keep your referral partners informed about the successes and outcomes of the clients they refer. This transparency builds trust and reinforces their confidence in your firm's ability to deliver excellent results.

Formalizing Referral Agreements

While informal referrals are valuable, formalizing your referral partnerships can provide clarity and structure to the relationship. This is best done through a referral agreement.

Elements of a strong referral agreement include:

Clear Terms: To start, define the expectations for both parties in the referral agreement. This could include the types of clients you're seeking, how referrals should be communicated, and the process for handling referred clients.

Incentives: Consider including incentives in your referral agreements, such as a referral fee or a reciprocal referral arrangement. Incentives often motivate your partners to prioritize referring clients to your firm.

Communication Protocols: Establish how and when you'll communicate about referred clients. This includes initial contact, updates on the client's case, and the final outcome.

Confidentiality: Ensure that all referral agreements include confidentiality clauses to protect the privacy of referred clients and maintain the integrity of your professional relationship.

By strategically building and nurturing a referral network, your firm can secure a steady stream of new clients, enhance its credibility, and achieve sustainable growth. These relationships will not only support your practice but will also amplify your impact within the community, ensuring that more individuals receive the legal guidance they need.

Key Takeaways

- **Identify Key Referral Sources:** Focus on clients, professionals, and organizations that are well-positioned to refer potential clients to your firm.
- **Provide Value to Partners:** Strengthen your referral relationships by offering educational resources, networking opportunities, and reciprocal referrals.
- **Network and Build Relationships:** Expand your referral network through consistent communication, one-on-one meetings, and collaborative projects.
- **Formalize Referral Agreements:** Create clear, structured agreements that outline the expectations, incentives, and confidentiality protocols for your referral partnerships.

Measuring Success: Key Metrics for Evaluating Firm Performance

A firm's success is so much broader than financial performance. It also involves measuring client satisfaction, operational efficiency, staff engagement, and the overall growth and health of your firm.

By carefully tracking key performance indicators (KPIs) across these dimensions, you can gain invaluable insights, pinpoint areas for improvement, and make strategic decisions that will propel your firm toward long-term success.

We've summarized each measure of success you should consider down below:

Client-Centric Metrics

Clients are The heart of any elder law and estate planning firm. As such, measuring client-centric metrics is crucial for understanding how well your firm is meeting client needs and expectations.

The most common metrics in this category include:

Client Satisfaction

Client satisfaction is a direct reflection of the quality of service your firm provides. To accurately monitor client satisfaction, implement surveys, feedback mechanisms, and track client reviews.

Regularly asking clients about their experience with your firm, the clarity of communication, and their overall satisfaction with the legal services provided can reveal how well you're building trust and delivering value — giving you the data necessary to optimize and enhance your processes later on.

Client Retention Rate

Another essential metric is the client retention rate, which measures the percentage of clients who continue to engage with your firm over time.

Tracking client retention over different periods can help identify patterns or trends. For example: A drop in retention rates might signal the need to revisit your client engagement strategies, communication protocols, or service offerings.

Operational Efficiency Metrics

Operational efficiency is about how well your firm utilizes its resources — primarily, its time, talent, and tools — to deliver legal services. Monitoring operational efficiency metrics helps you streamline processes, reduce costs, and increase profitability across every area of your firm.

Utilization Rate

Your firm's utilization rate is the percentage of billable hours or services actually used by your team members compared to the total available hours. A high utilization rate indicates that your team is working efficiently, with a significant portion of their time dedicated to billable work.

I do want to note that it's important to balance high utilization rates with employee well-being to avoid burnout. Personally, I recommend that firms regularly review this metric in conjunction with employee satisfaction to ensure your team is both productive and satisfied — ultimately leading to staff retention rates and reduced hiring costs over time.

Average Matter Profitability

Evaluating the profitability of individual matters or cases helps you understand which practice areas, services, or clients are most lucrative. By analyzing which types of cases yield the highest returns, you can make informed decisions about resource allocation, pricing strategies, and which services to expand or streamline.

Staff Engagement and Performance Metrics

A motivated and engaged team is vital for delivering high-quality legal services and maintaining a positive workplace culture. Monitoring staff engagement and performance metrics helps ensure that your team remains productive, satisfied, and aligned with the firm's goals.

Employee Satisfaction

Employee satisfaction is closely linked to productivity, retention, and overall firm culture. Regularly assess staff engagement and job satisfaction through surveys, feedback sessions, and performance reviews. High levels of employee satisfaction typically lead to increased productivity, reduced turnover, and a more positive work environment, all of which contribute to better client service.

Understanding the factors that drive satisfaction—such as opportunities for professional development, work-life balance, and recognition—can help you create a more supportive and motivating work environment.

Staff Utilization and Productivity

Monitoring staff utilization rates and productivity levels allows you to optimize workflow efficiency and resource allocation. By analyzing how time and resources are spent, you can identify bottlenecks, streamline operations, and ensure that your team is working effectively.

For example, if certain tasks are consistently taking longer than expected, it may indicate a need for additional training, better tools, or process adjustments. Regularly reviewing these metrics can help you maintain high productivity levels while also ensuring that staff workloads are manageable.

Growth and Financial Metrics

Growth and financial performance are traditional indicators of a firm's health and sustainability. Tracking these metrics helps you understand the financial viability of your firm and identify opportunities for expansion.

Revenue Growth

Revenue growth is a key indicator of your firm's financial health and its ability to attract and retain clients. By tracking revenue growth over time, you can assess how well your firm is performing financially and identify the sources of growth, such as new client acquisitions, increased service offerings, or higher client retention rates.

Analyzing revenue growth can also help you identify which areas of your practice are most profitable and where there might be opportunities for further expansion.

Profit Margin

Your firm's profit margin—the percentage of revenue that translates into profit after expenses—provides insight into cost efficiency and pricing strategies. A healthy profit margin indicates that your firm is managing costs effectively while still delivering valuable services at competitive rates.

Monitoring profit margins helps you evaluate the financial sustainability of your firm and make informed decisions about pricing, cost management, and investment in growth opportunities.

Continuous Improvement and Adaptation

In a rapidly changing legal landscape, continuous improvement and adaptation are essential for maintaining competitive advantage. By leveraging data and insights from your KPIs, you can drive continuous improvement and ensure that your firm remains agile and responsive to industry trends.

Data-Driven Decision-Making

Using data to inform decision-making allows you to identify trends, track progress, and make informed adjustments to your strategies. Regularly review and analyze performance metrics to adapt to changing market dynamics and client needs, ensuring that your firm stays on the cutting edge of the elder law and estate planning industry.

Benchmarking and Comparison

Benchmarking your firm's performance against industry standards, competitors, or previous performance metrics provides valuable context for your achievements and areas for improvement. Use benchmarking data to set goals, track progress, and identify best practices that can be implemented within your firm.

For example, if your firm's client satisfaction scores are below industry averages, you can explore what top-performing firms are doing differently and apply those strategies to improve your own client relationships.

Key Takeaways

- **Measure Success:** Measuring success in elder law and estate planning involves more than just financial metrics; it requires tracking client-centric, operational efficiency, staff engagement, and growth metrics.
- **Key Performance Indicators (KPIs):** Utilize Key Performance Indicators to gain insights into firm performance, identify areas for improvement, and drive strategic decision-making.
- **Continuously Improve:** Embrace a culture of continuous improvement by regularly reviewing performance data, benchmarking against industry standards, and adapting to evolving market and client needs.

Strategic Planning for Future Growth: Setting Goals and Roadmaps

Strategic planning is the bedrock of future growth and long-term success for elder law and estate planning firms. To navigate the complexities of the legal industry and seize opportunities as they arise, it's essential to establish clear goals, develop actionable roadmaps, and align your team around a unified vision. This structured approach ensures that your firm not only adapts to changes but also thrives in a competitive landscape.

Long-Term Vision

The foundation of any successful strategic plan is a well-defined long-term vision. This vision serves as your firm's North Star, guiding every decision and action over the next 5, 10, or 15 years. To craft this vision, consider the broader trends in the legal industry, shifts in client needs, advancements in technology, and emerging market opportunities. For example, if the demand for digital estate planning services is on the rise, your long-term vision might include becoming a leader in offering tech-driven solutions that simplify the estate planning process for clients.

This long-term vision should inspire and motivate your team, providing a clear picture of where the firm is headed and the impact it aims to make. It should also be flexible enough to accommodate unexpected changes in the market or industry, allowing your firm to adapt while staying true to its core mission.

SMART Goals

Once your long-term vision is in place, the next step is to break it down into Specific, Measurable, Achievable, Relevant, and Time-bound (SMART) goals. These goals transform your vision into actionable targets that guide your firm's day-to-day operations and strategic initiatives.

For example, if your long-term vision includes expanding your firm's market share, a SMART goal could be: "Increase market share by 15% within the next three years by expanding our service offerings to include Medicaid planning and launching targeted marketing campaigns." This goal is specific (focused on market share increase), measurable (15%), achievable (based on market analysis), relevant (aligns with the firm's growth strategy), and time-bound (within three years).

SMART goals provide a clear roadmap for success, helping your firm to stay focused and aligned with its strategic priorities.

Creating Actionable Roadmaps

Strategic Initiatives

To achieve your SMART goals, you need to identify key strategic initiatives—specific projects or actions that will move your firm closer to its objectives. These initiatives should be broken down into actionable steps, with each step clearly defined in terms of what needs to be done, who is responsible, and when it should be completed.

For example, if one of your SMART goals is to enhance client satisfaction, a strategic initiative might involve implementing a new client relationship management

(CRM) system. The actionable steps for this initiative could include researching CRM vendors, selecting the best fit for your firm, training staff on the new system, and launching it within a specific timeframe.

By clearly outlining these steps, you can ensure that everyone involved understands their role and the expected outcomes, which is crucial for maintaining momentum and achieving your strategic goals.

Resource Allocation

Achieving your strategic goals requires the effective allocation of resources, including financial investments, staff time, technology upgrades, and marketing efforts. It's important to prioritize initiatives that align most closely with your firm's strategic objectives and allocate resources accordingly.

For instance, if one of your goals is to increase your firm's digital presence, you might allocate resources to revamp your website, invest in SEO, and enhance your social media strategy. By aligning resources with strategic priorities, you can maximize impact and ensure that your firm is well-equipped to execute its plans successfully.

Aligning Team Efforts

Communication and Collaboration

Successful strategic planning hinges on the ability to align your team around common goals. This requires open communication, collaboration, and regular updates to keep everyone informed and motivated. Regular team meetings, progress reports, and transparent communication channels are essential for ensuring that all team members are on the same page.

Encourage collaboration by involving team members in the strategic planning process. When people feel that their input is valued, they are more likely to be engaged and committed to the firm's goals. This collaborative approach also fosters innovation, as diverse perspectives often lead to more creative solutions.

Cross-Functional Teams

Forming cross-functional teams can be a powerful way to drive strategic initiatives forward. By bringing together individuals with different expertise, you can leverage diverse skills and perspectives to tackle complex challenges more effectively. Cross-functional teams can also break down silos within the firm, fostering greater collaboration and knowledge sharing.

For example, if your firm is launching a new service offering, a cross-functional team might include attorneys, marketing professionals, IT staff, and client service representatives. This team would work together to develop the service, create marketing materials, and ensure a seamless client experience.

Monitoring Progress and Adaptation

Performance Tracking

Monitoring progress is critical to the success of any strategic plan. Establish key performance indicators (KPIs) for each goal and initiative and regularly review these metrics to track progress. KPIs would include client satisfaction scores, revenue growth, market share, or staff productivity.

Regularly reviewing performance data allows you to identify trends, spot potential issues early, and make data-driven decisions. If you notice that a particular initiative isn't delivering the expected results, you can adjust your approach before it negatively impacts your overall strategy.

Flexibility and Adaptability

While it's important to stay committed to your strategic goals, it's equally important to remain flexible and adaptable. The legal industry is constantly evolving, and your firm must be prepared to pivot when necessary. This might involve adjusting your goals, reallocating resources, or changing your approach to capitalize on new opportunities or mitigate risks.

For example, if a new regulation is introduced that affects estate planning practices, your firm may need to adapt its strategy to ensure compliance and continue delivering value to clients. Embracing a culture of agility and innovation will help your firm stay competitive and resilient in the face of change.

Celebrating Achievements and Learning from Challenges

Recognition and Appreciation

Celebrating successes along the way is vital for maintaining morale and motivation. Recognize and appreciate the contributions of individuals and teams that drive your firm's strategic goals. Celebrations can range from formal recognition at meetings to informal team gatherings, but the key is to acknowledge the hard work and dedication that lead to achievements.

Recognizing successes not only boosts morale but also reinforces the behaviors and practices that contribute to the firm's success. It shows your team that their efforts are valued and encourages them to continue striving for excellence.

Post-Implementation Reviews

After completing strategic initiatives, conduct post-implementation reviews to evaluate their effectiveness. Assess what worked well, what challenges were encountered, and what could be improved in future initiatives. These reviews provide valuable insights that can inform your next strategic planning cycle.

Learning from both successes and challenges is crucial for continuous improvement. By analyzing outcomes and capturing lessons learned, your firm can refine its strategic approach, avoid past mistakes, and build on its strengths.

Key Takeaways

- **Strategic Planning:** Strategic planning is essential for future growth and success, requiring clear goals, actionable roadmaps, and team alignment around a shared vision.
- **SMART Goals:** Establish SMART goals that are aligned with your firm's long-term vision and strategic priorities.
- **Roadmaps:** Create actionable roadmaps that include specific steps, resource allocation, and clear responsibilities to drive progress toward your goals.

- **Communicate & Collaborate:** Foster communication and collaboration to ensure that all team members are aligned and engaged in the strategic planning process.
- **Monitor & Adapt:** Monitor progress and remain adaptable, celebrating achievements and learning from challenges to continuously improve and sustain momentum.

CONCLUSION:
FUTURE-FOCUSED GROWTH

Building a future-focused elder law and estate planning firm is not a simple task — it's an exciting venture that requires dedication, foresight, and a willingness to embrace change. And, it's a journey that doesn't have a fixed endpoint. instead, it's an ongoing process of growth, learning, and adaptation.

The legal industry will continue to evolve, and your firm must evolve with it. This means staying informed about emerging trends, being open to new ideas, and continually seeking ways to improve your practice. It also means investing in your team's professional development, embracing new technologies, and refining your client service strategies to meet the changing needs of your clients — which we show you how to do in every page of this book.

But perhaps most importantly — it means staying true to your firm's core values and mission. In the face of change, these are the constants that will guide you. They are the principles that define who you are as a firm, how you serve your clients, and what you stand for in the legal community. As long as you remain committed to these values, you'll be able to navigate the challenges and uncertainties of the future with confidence and purpose.

So, I want to encourage you: Take time to celebrate the progress you've made so far. Building a successful elder law and estate planning firm is no small feat, and you should be proud of what you've accomplished. But don't lose sight of the work that lies ahead.

The road to success is long, and it's paved with continuous learning, adaptation, and improvement. Every step you take brings you closer to your goal of becoming a leader in the field, a trusted advisor to your clients, and a respected voice in the legal community.

As you continue to build your future-focused firm, know that you are not just shaping the success of your practice—you are making a lasting impact on the lives of the clients you serve.

Here's to a future filled with growth, innovation, and the unwavering pursuit of excellence in elder law and estate planning.

Your journey is just beginning, and the best is yet to come.

ABOUT BAMBIZ

At Bambiz, we understand the unique challenges estate planning and elder law attorneys face, and we're here to help you navigate them with confidence. Since 2016, we've been partnering with firms just like yours, providing innovative marketing strategies, cutting-edge technology, and hands-on guidance to help you achieve real growth.

We believe that building a successful, future-ready law firm requires more than just marketing—it's about creating a lasting connection with your community, building trust with your clients, and staying ahead of the curve with modern strategies. That's exactly what we offer:

- **Targeted Digital Marketing:** Whether it's social media management or high-converting ad campaigns, we help you attract the right clients and establish meaningful relationships.
- **Lead Generation Tools:** From webinars to seminars, we design and run powerful campaigns

that consistently bring in qualified leads and consultations.
- **Custom Websites and SEO:** We craft tailored, high-performing websites optimized to rank in search engines and attract local clients who are actively searching for your services.
- **Workshops and Educational Events:** Our workshops and seminars are a cornerstone of what we do. Known for delivering actionable insights, these events give attorneys the tools and knowledge they need to grow their practices and stay competitive.
- **Client Engagement and Retention:** We equip you with the right tools to keep your clients engaged and loyal, from effective email newsletters to reputation management strategies.

At Bambiz, we don't just offer services—we build lasting partnerships. Our team works closely with you to create a customized marketing strategy that fits your firm's specific goals and challenges. Together, we'll help you grow your practice, reach new clients, and ensure long-term success.

Ready to Learn More?

Visit www.bambiz.net to dive deeper into our services, explore success stories from other firms, and find out about our upcoming events. We'd love to talk about how we can partner with you to grow your practice and help you build the future-ready law firm you've always envisioned.

ACKNOWLEDGMENTS

Writing this book has been an incredible journey — one full of late nights, early mornings, and more coffee than I'd care to admit. It's been a rewarding process, and I'm excited to finally share the insights and strategies that have come from years of working alongside law firms across the country. But none of this would have been possible without the support of some amazing people.

First, to Andrea—you are the reason Bambiz exists. You brought me into this world of estate planning and elder law, and you've been by my side through every twist, turn, and idea along the way. Whether we're brainstorming the next big thing or you're reminding me to step away from my laptop, you've been my constant. Without your steady hand and support, I'd probably still be stuck chasing down a hundred different ideas. Thank you for keeping me grounded and for always being in my corner. I wouldn't want to do this with anyone else.

To Olivia—my source of endless energy and joy. You may not realize it yet, but you inspire me every day. Watching you grow reminds me of why it's so important to plan for the future. I hope you know that with hard work and passion, anything is possible.

To my family—you've been cheering me on from the very beginning. From those early, crazy ideas to the wins we've celebrated, you've always had my back. Your love and support have meant the world to me, and I'm grateful for everything you continue to give me.

To our clients—thank you for trusting us, not just with your marketing, but with your businesses and your vision. It's been an honor to walk this path with you, and we've shared the highs, the lows, and everything in between. If even one idea in this book helps you take your practice to the next level, then every long night has been worth it. Here's to more success, growth, and partnership in the years ahead!

To the Bambiz team—you're the heartbeat of this company. From the early days when it was just an idea to the impact we're making across the country today, you've been the ones turning vision into reality. Your creativity, dedication, and hard work have shaped Bambiz into what it is, and for that, I'm not just grateful—I'm proud to call you friends. Thank you for being an essential part of this journey.

And to the friends, mentors, and colleagues who have been there along the way—thank you for your advice, your support, and your willingness to listen when I needed it most. Your influence is felt on every page of this book, and I'm incredibly thankful for the role you've played in getting me here.

So, here's to all of you—thank you for being part of this journey, for helping me grow, and for making this book possible. Now, let's take what we've built and keep moving forward—there's still so much more to come.

Continue Your Journey with Free Bonus Materials

Your journey to building a future-ready law firm doesn't end here. Marketing, technology, and client relations are constantly changing, and we're committed to providing you with the latest tools and insights.

By scanning the QR code below, you'll unlock ongoing access to a library of bonus materials—including up-to-date strategies, video tutorials, and additional training. These resources are designed to help you continue adapting and growing your practice long after this book has been printed.

https://bambiz.net/future-ready-bonus

Made in the USA
Middletown, DE
17 February 2025